FINDING SELF-MOTIVATED ENGAGEMENT

In The Hyper Driven World-of-Work

Vinay Singh

CENTRAL PARK SOUTH PUBLISHING

Published by Central Park South Publishing 2022
www.centralparksouthpublishing.com

Typesetting and e-book formatting services by Victor Marcos

ISBN:
978-1-956452-12-9 (hbk)
978-1-956452-11-2 (pbk)
978-1-956452-16-7 (ebk)

This book is dedicated to Generation Z, and their development of soft skills, motivation and mentoring leadership for a better global society

TABLE OF CONTENTS

INTRODUCTION

Unfortunately, workforces around the world in the 21st century are deeply disengaged. People are simply unhappy at work for many reasons including: fear, stress, competition, politics, a growing lack of trust, and being underpaid, and underappreciated. I've seen all of this up front and personally. Throughout my career, I've been titled as a human capital leader but honestly, I often work in multiple capacities and through the lens of being a diversity professional and a social scientist, but everything I do is within technology too. Thus, I've gaining expertise in areas of technology talent acquisition, HR strategy, organization development and workforce transformation. During this time, I've worked in many technologies' disruption and socio-economic "waves" too; the end of mainstream mainframe technology as well as Y2K, convergence, wireless, the dotcom recession, the Great Recession of 2008, the boom of social media, the first iterations of AI/IOT, the start of AR/VR, the effects of Coronavirus and now our new virtual workforce and workplace.

Throughout my career, I've talked with countless candidates and thousands of corporate hiring personnel looking for the best candidates to hire and how to retain them. That's a long time to be advising people about what jobs are out there and listening to why they want to leave their current jobs. One thing has always been clear: there has been, and still is, a very high number of people who are disengaged with their work or workplace. From C-suite executives to friends and family, people have asked me why employees are so disengaged, and I tell them it could be one of a million reasons. Employees are sad, mad, they've been treated bad by their boss, their bosses' boss, their co-workers, by surprising new rules, established benefits taken away, by customers, by their peers, constant new management priorities; new rules, even by the government — the list goes on and on. As a result, they are unmotivated, bored, unhappy, stressed to the hilt, and driven to burn out.

Let's face it, we crush a lot more hours working than our parents or grandparents did. I remember hearing about the standard workday which was once nine to five. When I graduated in 1997, my dad was still working nine-to-five. Yet when I joined a tech recruiting firm after college, I was introduced to the hyper-speed of the dot-com era. On some days we still worked nine-to-five, but on other days we worked till 8:00 pm, and that was mandatory. If you wanted to produce high numbers, you worked longer hours. I certainly did, with many other colleagues. I even came in regularly on weekends to get ahead and try to get ahead of my previous month's quota record. While some folks were still working nine to five in the corporate world, it was easy to see the end of the nine-to-five workday was approaching rapidly. Today, does anyone work nine-to-five? Does anybody work forty hours a week and clock out every day at 5p.m. without having to, at the very least stop and acknowledge emails from co-workers or clients or a late-in-the-day memo from the boss, informing you of a very important 8 a.m. meeting the following morning? I'm sure people do; I just don't know many of those people.

With the faster pace of business today, comes more struggle to keep up and hence, anxiety for many people, most of whom are asked to stay later and produce more with very little additional support or compensation. In a lot of cases, they are also being asked to do this with inadequate technology, little advisory support, insufficient training, and in many cases, all three. Of course, almost everything is due *"yesterday"* too. Company goals today do not align properly with human productivity, and it's bringing the human psyche down. Add the fact that companies don't want to hire more people, nor give better wages unless they are forced to, yet they have billions in cash reserves and give hundreds of millions to corporate executives. This equation adds up to dissatisfaction at work.

Today's Workforce

Today, if you're entering the workforce, or even entered the workforce a few years ago, you are faced with all sorts of challenges. While you are part of the most tech savvy generation ever, you are also being catapulted into a world that moves much faster and changes more quickly than you ever experienced in college, graduate school, business school, or any other institution of learning that you ever attended. In many cases, what you learned in school is also not easily adaptable to real world situations. You may frequently find yourself saying, "wow, they never told us that in school."

To make it worse, the previously established path to success has been disrupted. You may even find yourself interviewing with employers who did not follow any "traditional" path at all. They have no business school credentials and, in some cases, not even a college degree. They took an entrepreneurial approach, one which has become more tempting in a world in which innovative online startups can become multi-million, and even multi-billion, dollar businesses. They succeeded because of positive thinking, learning (in or outside of a classroom) determination and hard work plus a host of "self-motivated" traits not taught in the vast majority of institutions.

These could be the people from whom you are looking for employment - they are the trendsetters that you want to learn from, work for, and eventually become. Their companies are engaging workplaces and, one day, you may be leading such a company as manager, CEO or founder/owner.

Motivation and Inspiration

Today, success stories come from anywhere and everywhere. For example, consider Shawn Corey Carter who grew up in the housing projects of Brooklyn's Bedford-Stuyvesant neighborhood. He felt disengaged back in high school, so he left to pursue his dream of becoming as a rapper. Carter created his own opportunities, which began when he took the letters of two Brooklyn subway lines (the J and the Z lines) and started rapping in any club that would have him. In time, Jay Z would become one of the most highly respected and influential artists of the 90s. But his dreams continued to expand as he built his own entertainment company called Roc Nation, opened a chain of 40/40 sports bars and even has part ownership of the Brooklyn Nets, while on his way to becoming hip-hop's first billionaire. He inspired many young people, especially in the African American communities, to follow their passion, and create their own opportunities, their own brands by constantly taking smart risks and branching out into new adventures.

Jay-Z is one of many examples of self-made success stories who seized opportunities when the path to the success was not spelled out in front of them. You can do that too by starting your career with the positive attitude that you will fulfill your dreams.

Then there are those people who are disenchanted by the way we treat our planet and, consequently, ourselves. They want to shake things up. Sarah Paiji Yoo, who had founded direct-to-consumer brands M. Gemi, Rockets of Awesome and Snappette, set out on a mission to find an eco-friendly cleaning product. Having taken time off from her career to spend with her newborn baby, she realized, while mixing baby formula with tap water, that tap water is contaminated with microplastics. To remedy this scary reality, she wondered if there was a dry tablet or powder that could be packaged in paper instead of plastic, which would allow anyone to reuse the same bottle again and again while not putting more and more plastic into our water supply.

When she found no such product, she decided to create one on her own and take it to market. Despite being turned down by more than 50 manufacturers, Yoo refused to cut corners or compromise her values. Ultimately, she decided to take on the challenge of starting her own company to sell her eco-friendly product.

Today, her company, Blueland, specializes in a host of eco-friendly cleaning products built on the idea that we don't have to sacrifice a clean planet for a clean home and for safer drinking water, unfettered by microplastics.

There are also motivational shining stars in major companies that we know quite well. For example, you probably already know of Sheryl Sandberg who has made her way up the ladder and is now working alongside Marc Zuckerberg as the COO of Meta. A best-selling author, Sandberg shows up on countless lists of the most influential people in the world. And to think, she left a job at Google after a chance meeting with Mark Zuckerberg at a 2007 Christmas event. Sandberg overcome her share of obstacles and controversies and ended up going from disengaged to very engaged and very wealthy too.

From a rap star turned business mogul, to an eco-friendly entrepreneur, to a woman who has risen to amazing heights in one of the most notable companies on the globe, all of these people had to start somewhere. Now it's your turn.

Feeling Engaged

One of my intentions of this book is for you to acquire the personal tools, such as the right mindset and positive attitude, to find a career in which you will feel happy and engaged. It's so important to enjoy what you do. Believe it or not, most people don't.

Let me give you some context over the past few years. In an article published by the Society for Human Resource Management (SHRM) in November 2017, Gallup statistics revealed that less than one-third of U.S. workers reported that they were "engaged" in their jobs. Of the country's approximately 100 million full-time employees, 51 percent say they were "not engaged" at work—meaning they felt no real connection to their jobs and tended to do the bare minimum. Another 17.5 percent were "actively disengaged"—meaning they resented their jobs, tended to gripe to coworkers, and dragged down office morale. Altogether, that's a whopping 68.5 percent of people who were not happy at work. These numbers are outrageous and unacceptable. And yes, all those statistics have become worse since the pandemic.

More recently, looking at the 2021 Gallup report, it states that "globally, employee engagement decreased by 2 points, from 22% in 2019 to 20% in 2020". Today, we are in historically disengaged times, so when you hear the 2021 term Great Resignation being used to describe the world's organizational hiring problems, hopefully you are starting to paint your own ideas of what and why we are in this disengaged state of today. Unfortunately, alcohol consumption, depression, loneliness and financial hardship are just some of the many growing problems that continue to persist in 2022.

Part of the problem is that many corporate leaders don't seem to know what's important to employees. Some need to be replaced because either they don't know what's going on, some they simply don't care – or both! Leaders need to engage their employees, with good communication about what work needs to be done, *and* why it needs to be done. People are more engaged when they have a reason for showing up. In addition, it's important for leaders and managers to be transparent about the business in which these employees spend a large chunk of their time every week. They also need to respect their employees as people and recognize that they have needs and concerns outside of the office and deserve a fair work life balance, which means not keeping them at the office until 8 o'clock at night, and that means not having to answer emails too.

For decades, companies didn't focus on employee experience and engagement as a priority—they've lost sight of that part of the employee equation, largely because of the obsession with technology and hyper-speed need of everything. Employers need to take a step back and realize that people are still the best producers of great work and work environments. Getting the latest technology will not make your business great, ONLY the people will. Many companies fail to understand this basic reality, and as a result, they spend millions of dollars upgrading technology and little to nothing on training and re-skilling their greatest asset, and consistently lose good people.

In This Book

While there are many external reasons to feel disengaged at work, some of which we've mentioned earlier in the chapter, such as the economy, uninspiring leadership and/or working with little training and poor tools, we can't solve all of the possible reasons behind a feeling of disengagement. Yes, you can go out and look for a better job, but there's no guarantee that the environment, your new manager, the business owner, or even the culture of the new business environment will make you feel involved and engaged. Therefore, while you may not be able to change the environment, you can take it upon yourself to make the necessary changes that will put you in a position to self-induce engagement, either at your current position, or at your next job.

With that in mind, this book is largely about acquiring the tools to be positively engaged and actively motivated to reach your goals. This includes potentially taking on the challenge of self-improvement and building the determination to succeed. If you are shining with positivity and bring your A-game attitude to work every day, your new ability to provide happiness, inspiration and motivation to your customers, clients, and co-workers will result in them wanting to work with you more often. As a result, you will feel better about yourself and won't fall into that massive negative pool of disengaged employees. In fact, you'll feel engaged in your work and may be singled out in a positive way. Yes, everyone will want to be around you and work with you because you will now be both engaged at your job and seen as a high performer, which could put you at the top of the list for the next promotion.

Mastering personal motivation and engagement is a factor we can personally control – but you will not get there using an app or by taking a quick Massive Open Online Course (MOOC), which are short online courses that are popping up all over the place. Truth is that nothing worthwhile comes easily so I won't make any promises or offer any guarantees. How you come into the office or approach working remotely is in your control.

In the upcoming sections I will present many self-motivational lessons set up by category to include ideas that you can apply to your personal work and to your environment. They will be the foundation for you to build a personal set of work attitudes and a mindset that will help you get the most out of your workday and guide you in building your career.

The goal is to be engaged at work, so much so, that if you happen to work your way up to a leadership role, or start your own business, you will focus on having motivated, happy people that are accountable to each other. You won't be one of those leaders that just gives orders but instead you will be a natural motivator, who has the ability and vision to see talent in their people as well as where their people need help – and actually help them. Incidentally, this trait is a lost part of the criteria of being a manager today. I love this quote from Elbert Hubbard, *"There is something that is much scarcer, something finer far, something rarer than ability. It is the ability to recognize ability."* That ultra-rare ability is a powerful human gift that the world's best corporate executives, those who lead by example, have. You also see it in the best sports coaches who propel their teams to championships over and over again with new personnel, there are also incredibly talented psychology coaches that work to better people and yes, there are those inspiring teachers you remember, if you're lucky, from your years in school.

One of the other reasons why I wrote this book was to provide something that is so rare in the world today – mentorship. The lack of mentorship these days is another major reason why people are disengaged.

Zenger Folkman, a provider of leadership programs, states that the trait that would have an overwhelming impact on an organization's performance. It is "the ability of leaders to inspire and motivate others.

Yet when leader's traits are scored, these traits are consistently among the lowest traits on the list." The good news is that behaviors that make leader's inspiring can be studied and practiced resulting in new founded heights for performance. My goal, and this book, is to provide those bits and pieces of wisdom that will help you excel in your chosen career. Ultimately, this book aims to teach the qualities of self-motivated engagement so you too can potentially become a strong leader, an entrepreneur and/or a mentor if you so desire.

Read, take notes, and re-read the sections that apply most to you. You'll find as your life and priorities change, this book can continue to meet your goals as you grow. Enjoy.

Chapter 1

The Way You Think is Everything

The Difference Between Good and Great Is How You Think

What's the difference between good and great? It comes down to how you think – plus having a positive attitude helps enormously. We all identify with certain famous people; they were childhood role models, and even as we get older, we find people to admire. Often these people went through some real tough times. But we admired how they kept plugging away and never gave up. When they got their moment to shine, they took advantage of it, and did something that put them on the map of fame or success.

. . . .

What You Think About Is What You Create

Vision becomes reality: If you want to be great at something, look at what you're currently doing and where you can make the difference to change something. Then focus on and work on that change repeatedly. Watch it come to fruition.

Let me give you an example: during my career in staffing account management, a part of my job was a numbers game – the more people I reached out to, the more chances I would get someone to respond and work with me. It's a sales 101 metric that has stood the test of time. So, I thought about it, and decided that if I worked more hours than everyone else, I could make a difference in my career. I moved close to work, got up early every Saturday morning and went into the office from 9a.m. to 1p.m. I used to sleep late and watch T.V. during that time. I made a career decision and an adjustment to change my schedule to a new one. I followed that routine for two full years. It turned me into a million-dollar producer, which was a very big deal, at that time there was only one other person in the six branch offices who had that title and she had three times more years of experience than I did. I'm not recommending that you do what I did, I'm saying find what works for you and create your own destiny.

Success starts from within: Maximize your potential by doing little things to "feel successful" while you are on your quest and goals. Something I liked doing was after every successful deal I made, I'd read a famous quote on sales and leadership and contemplate how it pertained to...ME! It's a great individual boost, what you think of yourself is everything!

Attitude is a habit: Bottom line, people who look at the glass as half empty have developed negativity as a habit. It affects the actions they take and the life patterns they find themselves in. But negative habits can be replaced by focusing on taking the negative and creating something new to combat it and then focusing and working on that something new.

Don't let a crisis turn you negative: How many times have we heard about someone in history who fought atrocities we would not want to imagine having to endure? History is filled with folks subjected to unbelievable abuse. One way to stay positive and on the right track is to identify with someone who went through something you admire and always keep them as a reminder as to what you are going through in times of a rut. For me, I keep framed photos of the people I admired and also pictures of people I don't' know but have gone through things I would never wish on anyone. It reminds me that what I'm experiencing isn't as bad; it reminds me that I've got a much better chance of surviving what I am going through and also, gives me perspective. How I react needs to be the best I can make it.

Trust your Gut for Success—But You've Also got to Believe

You can't think your way to success until you learn to trust your gut—even when that means flying in the face of doubt or failure. For me personally, in agency (commissioned) talent acquisition, if I didn't trust my gut and believe in myself, I'd never go into a new client business development meeting and walk out with a signed contract to do business. We all know in sales; you've got to have confidence; that is requisite 101. Obviously, if you never get a client, you'll never get the chance to produce exceptional results for that client, establish a strong relationship and become a trusted advisor. You've got to make promises about your ability to deliver and yes, sometimes you'll fail, but more times than not you'll deliver. Bottom line here is that before you can promise and trust your gut you've got to believe in yourself.

I recall my first job in recruiting. In a boutique privately held staffing agency, we had six small teams broken into specific technology niches. Shortly after I joined the agency, I was promoted to a manager role, and soon I'd be hiring my first team member to mentor and manage.

Back then I put a lot of time into getting ahead. I was often the person who closed the office doors, the last one out. Laser-focused to succeed, I rarely did the talk at the water cooler; I walked into the office with a game plan and boom—I went right to my desk to start my day. I knew people thought I had an attitude because I didn't spend time chatting. I walked around with a "quick step" in my walk; I was always focused on what I was doing. I'll also never forget a work colleague telling me, "Hey man, I don't know why you are in such a hurry. You are the sixth manager here and the newest. Around here it's tenure and that's how you move up. So, you're not getting to branch manager any time before me or the people who are here before me."

I thought, "If I work harder than everyone else and consistently outperform everyone, would the president of this company really not promote me over the others? That didn't make sense to me; that went against what I've been taught."

Sure enough, three years later, when the company split because we grew so big, everyone in the company either had to work for me or for Kim, who had been the first manager hired and a family member of the president. I trusted my gut, I believed I knew what was right because it made sense to me. Take the time to realize what makes you unique. What makes you stand out? What is different in your approach to that of your colleagues? Or maybe you want to do something different but haven't because it goes against the grain of the culture. Yet, you know it could be the difference maker and it feels right to you.

Success starts with attitude and confidence in your decisions. Do your homework. Weigh your options. Then choose a direction and act on it – don't procrastinate. In the end, that's how some of your best decisions will be made.

Positive Thinking: Focus on Winning

At a young age, I heard about how athletes would imagine themselves crossing a finish line and winning their races. Since I daydreamed and read comic books as a kid, I had a pretty good imagination. I would imagine the things I wanted to achieve when I got older. So, when I learned about visualization, which is the process by which you imagine success and focus on your tasks and outcomes, I gravitated towards it, and used it as a tool for my success.

Years later, after graduating college and working around the clock to achieve successes in the corporate world, many people in my company would ask me, "Vinay, how do you do it. How do you always get the deal done?" I would tell them about the technique called *visualization*. I'd tell them "By picturing success and figuring out ways to avoid repeating mistakes and seeing it in your mind, that's how you perform visualization." When describing deal making with my employees, I'd describe it similar to this: You go over scenarios in your mind, and as you are perfecting each nuance of how your business opportunity can go, you picture your outcomes and play them out in your mind – and learn to make them a reality. As you practice this technique, you'll start to close many opportunities as you envision them. You'll also start to close more deals than you lose, because you're preparing for how things will go. Do that for a year and see how successful it works for you.

Visualization is a good tool to help you overcome obstacles throughout your career. You can also use visualization to look back at your mistakes and picture how you might have done things differently. Rather than making excuses for failure; the key is learning from mistakes and visualizing where you went wrong. By replaying what went wrong in your mind, many times, and then preparing to do things differently next time, you will be able to learn from your mistakes instead of repeating them. That's how I made visualization a success for me. Have you ever heard Einstein's famous saying, "Doing the same thing over and over, expecting different results is the definition of insanity?" If you repeat the same mistakes over and over again in the business world, you're not going to have a very good career.

One of the key components of visualization is staying positive. You need to be prepared for several things that can derail your positivity such as the following:

Fear: Know that most of the things that we fear will never manifest. Remember that the only one person who can control your fear is you.

Worry. When we worry, we reprogram our minds focusing on positivity and success to a mindset that prepares for failure or disaster, which quite frankly create a host of negative emotions and behaviors. It's important to remember that worrying does not solve anything. In fact, we often worry about thinks that don't happen.

Doubt: It's easy to doubt what we cannot see, touch, or smell. Don't let your thinking get the better of you. Focus on your positive beliefs.

Experts say: "Our thoughts lead to our discussions, which lead to our beliefs, which lead to our decisions, which lead to our actions."

Staying Cool Under Pressure Is Key to Success.

We all get nervous in high-pressure situations. Whether you're a star athlete throwing a pass with one-minute left on the clock, an executive giving bad news to the board, or someone interviewing for his or her dream job, walking the high wire can get to you.

According to motivational coaches who work with Olympic athletes, the difference between Olympic champions and the rest of us is that they've learned how to stay cool and focused when the pressure is on. They don't panic when they get nervous – they use specific strategies to keep their nerves under control. Many of them use their anxiety to push themselves to even greater heights."

Expect Nervousness: The secret to dealing with nervousness is to expect it. Recognize that it's normal to get nervous in competition or when you're being evaluated. Being nervous can help you concentrate more sharply and it can make you react faster because you've been preparing for it; therefore, you can be ready and have the energy when you need it. It's all in how you react.

Writers who interview Olympic champions are always asking questions like, "How do you stay calm before a meet?" Often the responses from Olympians are similar. They often say things like, "I'm nervous, sure. But that's exactly what I want to feel." Successful athletes accept nervousness as a natural part of the competitive process—and you should too."

Prevent Panic: Sometimes, though, even the most experienced competitors lose their cool. During a performance you don't have a lot of time to respond to the challenges thrown at you. In a sales presentation, a customer suddenly asks you a difficult question for which you are completely unprepared. Or how about during an interview for a job, when you are asked about a scenario that you've never encountered before? In these situations, it's natural and common that people make mistakes. This is the moment when you need to respond most effectively.

· ·

Tips to prevent panic and stay cool under pressure

Stay focused: The simplest technique is to focus on performance. When you are fully focused and paying attention to your performance, then you're in the flow and fully engaged. You can react automatically. Stop worrying about others or how you may appear. Your thinking will be clearer and your responses will be automatic. It's impossible to focus if your mind is racing. If you are thinking about other things, like your next appointment or meeting, you are not focused.

Performance cues: Creating performance cues is all about preparation. A performance cue can be a visual image as well as a verbal reminder to make you think of something you want to remember. Think of them ahead of time. Break them into short phrases. Rehearse them often—don't wing it. The essence of an effective cue is that it directs attention to something that enhances the chances of your success.

Creating the win: As an area manager and branch manager, I made sure I led by making decisions geared toward doing right by client and candidate no matter what. Often that meant taking money out of my personal deals to show my subordinates that money was not everything, doing the right thing was. When you lead, whether it's a team, or a project, let your troops see you taking the high road. Lead decisively, think on behalf of everyone's best interest and lead with emotional intelligence.

Michael Jordan on Positive Thought and Overcoming Obstacles

Basketball great Michael Jordan learned from the greats—and then set out to beat them. "I built my talents on the shoulders of someone else's talents." Without Julius Erving, David Thompson and Walter Davis, there would have never been a Michael Jordan. "I evolved from them," Jordan wrote in his book, *For the Love of the Game.*

Those guys presented a challenge, something to improve on. "I had the idea I had to be better than Julius Erving, Magic Johnson. Those were the guiding forces in my development, and I used them as motivation," said Jordan.

Overcoming Obstacles: A great turnaround came for Jordan when he conquered his greatest failure, fear: fear of failure, fear of looking bad, and fear of disapproval. "I think fear sometimes comes from a lack of focus or concentration, especially in sports. If I had stood at the free-throw line and thought about ten million people watching me on the other side of the camera lens, I couldn't have made anything," he recalled. "So, I mentally tried to put myself in a familiar place. I thought about all the times I shot free throws in practice and went through the same motions, the same technique that I had thousands of times. You forget about the outcome. You relax and perform."

If you can see fear of failure as a mirage then you've cleared half the hurdles, Jordan says. You may think something is standing in your way, "but nothing is really there," except a chance "to do your best and gain some success."

For Jordan, failure became fuel. "Sometimes it actually just gets you closer to where you want to be," he said. "When I got cut from the varsity team as a sophomore in high school, I learned something. I knew I never wanted to feel that bad again. I never wanted to have that taste in my mouth, that hole in my stomach," he recalls. "I decided to become a starter on the varsity team. That's what I focused on all summer. When I worked on my game, that's what I thought about. When it happened, I set another goal, a reasonable manageable goal that I could realistically achieve if I worked hard enough," Jordan said.

He was determined to be number one, but he wasn't in a hurry to get there. "I approached everything step by step," he said. He boosted his confidence by setting and achieving short term goals. "Each time I visualized where I wanted to be, what kind of player I wanted to become. I gained a little confidence every time I came through."

It's no wonder that so many business leaders can relate to Michael Jordan and take these messages into their own company, department, and teams. I know I can take these messages into my work environment where they motivate me and my coworkers to stay focused on small wins to achieve ultimate goals.

In the business world, this could occur when you are in the work environment heading into a meeting with much higher-level personnel. You want to embrace the moment and make sure to get everything you can from the meeting. You may even want to do the unthinkable and turn your phone off! Tell yourself to concentrate on everything that each person talks about, and pay attention to details and even try making eye contact.

Let that person know you are focused on what they are saying. You should also have a pen and paper with you to write down any ideas so you can build on what people who have achieved a higher status in your company have done. If Michael Jordan can do it, so can you!

Program yourself to be more positive

Change the way you think, and you can change your life. What do all optimists have in common? They see setbacks as temporary. They realize that events are not life-changing. It's how one reacts to those events that can be. *And reacting optimistically is a skill that can be learned and self-taught.*

If we can see that events are isolated and temporary—for example, "My boss didn't like my report, not because it wasn't done well or I didn't follow instructions, but rather she disagreed with a few of the points I raised"—then we can accept constructive viewpoints and the future can remain positive.

Do you want to be more optimistic? One way to improve your outlook is through *disputing*. You do this by playing positive messages in your mind while facing problems or criticism. You must remind yourself that the setback you're facing is short-term and easy to repair.

Consider these four factors to determine if you are inclined to be optimistic or pessimistic. This research is endorsed by Guggenheim Foundation and MacArthur Foundation:

Maternal influence: There's a correlation between the way your mother talked to you when you were a kid, and talked in general, and your own self-talk—optimistic or pessimistic.

Influential adults: The way teachers, coaches, and other influential adults spoke to you when you were younger—particularly when you failed—influences the way you see yourself and the way you react to circumstances.

Events early in life: If events that were permanent and unchangeable occurred, like a family member dying before you were ten, you tend to become pessimistic. If they were changeable, like your father going off to war and coming back, you tend to be more optimistic.

Events in adolescence and young adulthood: Major events occurring in your teens or early twenties affect the way you perceive events later in life. These could be achievements or setbacks in high school or college—and the role you played in them.

These factors form what is called the *explanatory style*. This is the way we think and explain events to ourselves. Those who explain events positively resist depression at up to eight times the rate of those with pessimistic views, studies show.

Ultimately, optimistic folks do better at work and have better physical health, too.

Building a Powerful Foundation Mindset

I remember when I was in elementary school my dad made me write down any mistake I had in my English and grammar homework 11 times. I remember hating it but also never understanding why he chose the number "11." Eventually my mom told me that my grandfather made my dad write everything that he got wrong 11 times and said back then it was a lot harder because "he had a lot less tools and resources; he grew up in a poor village in India – "so I should be thankful". I remember those days well because I wrote so much, due to the fact that I got a lot wrong when I was young! But you know what? By the time I got to Middle School I also remember that during in-class reading sessions I helped my fellow classmates a lot when they couldn't figure out words. I also remember teachers telling my parents about it during parent-teacher sessions; they told my parents that I was an exceptional student, which made them, and me, very happy.

My own story reminds me of the former CEO of the Fortune 500 company, PepsiCo Corporation, Indra Noori. I learned that when Indra was a little girl and her paternal grandfather asked her to do something and she didn't he would make her write "I will not make excuses", which I thought was funny until I found out she had to write it 200 times! When Indra grew up though, she also was grateful for the hard lessons of making mistakes and writing. Consider how both of these lessons constructed a mindset for not making mistakes and that the consequences that can follow. It makes you work harder and pay more attention to your work.

There is also another powerful lesson in Indra's childhood that I want to point out. As a little girl Indra grew up in India in a town called Madras, in a rather conservative family. Her mother had a major impact on her as well because every night at dinner time her mother asked her and her sister to write a speech about what they would do if they were somebody very important like a president or a prime minister and each night it was to be a different leader. She and her sister had to make each night's speech about something about what was happening with how they felt that day. And, to throw a little competition into it, she and her sister voted who had the better speech and that person was the winner for the night – clearly, they had fun with it while also creating a special bond between a mother and her daughters. Later in life, Indra realized that the confidence and the mindset she developed as a child is what she credited helping her achieve an MBA from Yale in 1980 and helped her build a very successful career in jobs at Johnson & Johnson, Boston Consulting and eventually working with Jack Welch at GE on her way up to becoming CEO of PepsiCo.

What I found most powerful is the foundational reinforcement that this kind of activity and process creates. You may have heard the saying "practice makes perfect." Well, in our hyper chaotic lives, there's less of that opportunity and fewer people supporting this in each of our lives. Today, you have to be involved in your own leader development more than ever and that is why I have brought up this learning lesson. Such reinforcement is what I want to steer you towards, which helps you develop a powerful "whatever it takes" mindset. A powerful positive mindset is critical as it shapes the way you think and how you see everything and it will carry you through life and in times of stress, and times of tribulation. It will affect how you think and will help you construct the path for each and every stage of your life.

You're not alone in needing to develop a powerful and positive mindset, we all need it, from writers to CEO or whatever you dream of becoming in the future. You need a powerful positive mindset if you are to become all that you dream you can be. Developing this mindset, you can have it too.

Focus on your passions: Make sure you support yourself by focusing on the things you love. Now that may sound logical, but it can be tough to do as well. For example, you may have family and peer pressure to do something other than what you love. You may also feel like you have no choice. Just remember that you might have to do some things you don't want, even if it means keeping the things you love to do on the side. It's those kinds of things that make your day worthwhile.

For example, I was never encouraged to explore my love and interest in classic American muscle cars, but I always read about them and enjoyed writing about them as well. Well, after I graduated college, I started to collect them and wouldn't you know it, I eventually became a member and board leader of a large national car club and I've even been featured as a guest editor of a magazine. Not sure what your true passions are? Start with journaling. Keep it in your bedroom so you can get to it every morning and every night. Write your thoughts down and I promise, it will come to you!

Slow down the speed of your emotions: this is not easy to do! Do not be hard on yourself if you struggle at first, but as mentioned above, focus on remembering this and you can make it happen. When you catch yourself thinking negatively, tell yourself stop! Then, take a deep breath. Try intentional breathing 3 to 5 times. Tell yourself that isn't what you are going to do to yourself anymore. Practice becoming more mindful when negative thoughts come to you. These thoughts come because you're thinking and behaviors have, unfortunately become automatic. But it can be reversed. You can do it with practice.

Don't ever give up growing and that means change: You've heard winners never quit, right? Wrong! Yes, winners quit – they quit bad habits and they quit doing things that don't work. You too can also make the choice to do better things too, if you are willing to admit you might have made a bad choice and self-correct. It's your life and it's the only one you have. You're only fooling yourself if you choose to continue doing something you don't want to. Your time is now.

Chapter 2

Environment, Culture and Workplace

Environment is a key to success

Look at the people around you, on and off the job. Do they lift you up or pull you down? How do you respond to them? What is the environment around you like; motivating or frustrating?

I spent a good part of my career as a professional staffing services director catering to financial services clients on Wall Street. It's a position where I always had to meet and exceed high customer and candidate demands. Imagine trying to keep your candidate's optimism up during the worst days, months and years of both of the first two U.S. recessions of this century - the dotcom crash and 2008! It was the same during COVID and will be just the same in certain coming years, I can assure you. When I was a working for these client organizations, no matter how I felt, I had to uphold the spirit of optimism and steadiness. I was also focused on hiring very positive people to create an enthusiastic environment. At one of my employers, we held "reward parties;" which were celebrations for the employee who performed exceptional for the week and also for the month. They seemed as common as coffee breaks when times were good but also when times were super tough. It was the great way to keep our team's emotional happiness up after a sometimes-brutal week of clients saying no, no, no to all the candidates we sent over. But I also had very supportive bosses who encouraged these celebrations. I can tell you, I've worked in environments where it was the opposite, where management was watching every penny, and it was all work and no engagement. I didn't last long in those environments; quite frankly neither did the people around me either. Have you ever been in that kind of work environment? You know the kind: where it seems like everyone is looking for their next job.

Many attributes come from a positive and upbeat environment:

Achievement: An upbeat environment not only motivates individuals but promotes teamwork. People achieve for personal gain as well as for the good of their department or the company as a whole. The outcome is a real energy you can feel.

Creativity: A positive environment creates brainstorming. Brainstorming encourages new ideas. Mentors and mentees share their experiences. Suggestions are encouraged and put to the test. When suggestions work, people are rewarded and spotlighted.

Support: When things go wrong, pointing fingers is out; collective problem solving is in.

That which holds true during the work day applies to after hours as well. The point is, if you are encouraged in your work environment, the environment will rub off on you and you'll be a person that is encouraging others everywhere you go. It's infectious!

Being in positive environments and around positive people will encourage you. Negative environments and negative people will not. Seek out those in your network and in your personal life who are positive. For example, are there people who you can talk to in other parts of your organization? Maybe there are people who you collaborate with from other departments? Is your manager someone you get along with? Are you part of any Meetup or LinkedIn groups that you have not engaged much in but you could reach out to some new people in those groups? These are some examples of opportunities you can spend more time cultivating and communicating with folks to generate a positive pool of people who support you. Seriously, try to do it in person or by video chat (but not text) and get comfortable enough to be able to bounce ideas off of them. Assertiveness comes from confidence; aggression often comes from anger. If you are assertive, you act; if you are aggressive, you react. Make every effort to reduce the negative and surround yourself with the positive people and watch yourself flourish.

Positive Values Breed a Positive Culture

Companies with a positive environment can usually trace their culture of good feelings to a basic value that drives them. Whether the value is humility, decisiveness, or open communication, company leaders must stress it often. The truth is, you don't need to be leading a company or even a team to benefit from focusing on your positive values and how you can use them to motivate yourself and even those around you.

Good Company Values Equal Happy Employees: I worked at an organization that had the most unique organizational structure for a company in which we all got paid by how hard we worked together as a team and our compensation was tied to each other. This was how the company was built, on foundational concrete values: teamwork and trust. It worked and it proved to be amazing. Never had I felt so much happiness and motivation, or achieved more success than when I was in that environment. It was a brilliant corporate structure that I've never seen since.

Today, I hear about teammates who are often working against each other to some degree; sometimes I even hear about environments where there are systems in place to instill the desire to help your colleagues achieve greater success too. The model I was exposed to had this idea that the more you helped someone succeed, the more you were rewarded. You had genuine interest in seeing your teammates achieve the highest possible success because your pay was tied to their success. The company fostered an amazing culture of doing right by your peers. The end result was we all made tons of money and personally I slept like a baby, knowing our coworkers had each other's back. It's no wonder we all enjoyed coming to work, staying late, and laughing so much.

Working in a Negative Environment: Working in a negative environment is probably one of the most disengaging things an employee can face. To know that you are going to work every day in a place that you don't care for (or dread), that just starts your day off wrong. I think we all can agree that an employee's creativity rises and falls depending on attitude. An environment you look forward to going to every day puts you in a happier, "ready-to-innovate" frame of mind. When attitude is right, creativity and positivity are high. As a manager of people, I always try to develop an environment that's self-critical and challenging. I encourage my team members to have a voice, one where they are not afraid to speak up, even about our environment or what we are doing.

I've worked in opposite environments where folks locked up their desk when they went to the bathroom or lunch. Those environments had such high turnover. Seriously, people would literally get up to go use the bathroom and never come back. I would go to lunch or leave for home on Friday, and that might be the last time I ever saw that person. At one company, you'd never even get to meet some folks. I remember asking a coworker one time, "Hey what happened to that new guy who started in so and so's group last week?" The answer was, "heard he went for a coffee break last Thursday, no one's seen him since."

You don't want to work in that environment. Having a trusting corporate culture, an open communication workplace is where it's at.

Building Trust in the Workplace

An environment of trust in the workplace is a key element in carrying a company forward, especially in times of change. Employees and mid-level managers need to know where they stand with the leaders at the top.

Everyone wants a positive workplace environment, but achieving it is impossible without high levels of credibility. Change can erode the credibility of even the best-intentioned leadership teams. Whether the change is a leveraged buyout, merger, or constantly changing technology systems, the result is often a lack of stability among workers. Instability leads to tension and often a lack of trust. That is why building trust is key to success and especially today in the constantly changing world of work.

Imagine coming to work every day wondering whether your job will change, your work team will change, or the company itself will change. Often, management could clear the air by just being up-front and honest.

Change, however, isn't the only cause of decreased trust. Whenever information on key issues is held back from employees, you increase levels of distrust and suspicion. People wonder what is really going on. When that happens, low trust levels among the staff will reduce productivity, decrease motivation, and hurt (management's) decision-making process, because the work force isn't really behind decisions. Symptoms of low credibility include high turnover; increased absenteeism; and an "active rumor mill."

When it comes to building trust, here are some best practice tips from top experts:

Be consistent: Make your values and mission statement your personal code of conduct.

Provide information: Offering accurate information in a timely manner will boost trust levels almost immediately.

Give employees more control: If you're in a management or leadership position, whether or not your company is undergoing change, give your workers as much freedom as possible to achieve goals and do their jobs.

Show the people working around you that they are valued: Don't arbitrarily make decisions that affect people negatively.

Look for solutions: When problems crop up, don't assign blame. Make sure that problem solving is a positive team effort company-wide.

Build teams and relationships: The most effective leaders are team players. Value teamwork, and promote an environment that encourages relationships among coworkers.

Poll Links Workers' Attitudes to Revenues

Positive attitudes in the workplace are giving companies a leg up in four key areas, a Gallup poll reveals. Companies whose workers have a positive attitude about their jobs are reporting higher profits, revenues, and productivity—and lower turnover rates—than those whose employees are negative. Worker attitude was measured by queries about twelve aspects of work:

1. Understanding of employee's duties (based on management input).
2. Access to needed materials.
3. Opportunity to excel daily.
4. Recognition of good work during the previous seven days.
5. Personal interest shown by supervisor or coworkers.
6. Career development encouraged by supervisor.
7. Employee input encouraged by supervisor.
8. Importance of employee's job as viewed by management.
9. Commitment of coworkers to doing the best job possible.
10. Environment that fosters friendship at work.
11. Employee progress tracked by one or more people every six months.
12. Opportunity to learn and grow during the previous year.

Revenues are 29 percent higher and productivity rates 50 percent greater at companies whose work forces are positive, according to the Gallup Organization. The poll was part of a two-year study, surveying 100,000 workers in twelve industries. Industries ranged from health care and education to retail, entertainment, and telecommunications. Firms were categorized into groups by sector and size; then each group was divided into four quarters based on average attitude rating of employees.

Bottom Line Results: Over two years, companies in the top quarter of each group produced on average 44 percent higher profits and 29 percent greater revenues than firms in the lowest tier. Productivity was 50 percent higher and turnover 13 percent lower at top-tier firms than at companies in the bottom quarter.

The poll, which surveyed 2,500 business units, showed that profitability and other key measures—tied to employee attitudes—can vary widely from one company division to another.

"What we find is that one company does not mean one culture," said a Gallup consultant. "Rather, there are as many cultures within a company as there are front-line managers." A practice leader with the Gallup Organization agrees. "We are simply in a new era… Machines don't matter—minds do. And to be successful, companies must engage the mind, talents, and attitude of each employee."

Chapter 3

Aspiring Leadership

Think Positively and Lead by Example

Top business people are widely recognized as positive people, both in the office and outside of the office. In fact, throughout the years, in poll after poll of the nation's top-performing publicly-traded firms, executives see themselves as positive thinkers according to national surveys from organizations like the Institute of Policy and Politics. But it's not enough for business leaders to think positively today. They need to set a positive tone company wide. For example, positive leaders do many things such as praise their employees, identify and point out when they do good work and create an enthusiastic environment. But, they also do more than that – for example, being the role model of the team. One of the best practices I used to set the tone of my team's culture was leading by example.

My motto was, "I have to be able to do everything I expect my employees to do – and do it well." I trained my staff, and I'd tell them: if I can do it, you can do it too. But if you just say it, then it's just words—I would show them that I could do it. As they watched me do things they were confused about, I'd watch them say "A-ha! Now I get it." I also let them know that they can put aside their fear of not succeeding because they will have the support and encouragement when they fall down, and I would be there to help them get back up. In other words, they can risk making a mistake and it's ok.

For example, I had situations in which a candidate was looking for $180K in compensation but the offer from the company came back at $175K and they told me that they can't budge and in fact they would move to their second-choice candidate if mine would not agree by the end of business day. I would make a case to my candidate on the $175k by emphasizing the benefits, the culture and the other personal reasons why it would make sense for the candidate to not miss out on the opportunity associated with the position. A new recruit on my team could see how I found I explained the additional benefits and reasons to make up for the difference in pay and presented this new package to the candidate. By seeing me in action and hearing my ability to craft situations and influence others, he or she could now have a better grasp of how I did things and how they too can do it. This is why it's so important for new employees to "shadow" their managers and follow their mannerisms, it's why shadowing can be very effective in mentoring in any number of professional fields.

Years ago, leaders were more hands-on and because of that, younger employees were shown how to do things.

Today, we sit in front of a computer and are self-taught. But that doesn't mean if you have a question, you're going to get an answer. Computers don't talk back, yet, and now you have to go searching for an answer - do you have the time to do that extra research? How often is the answer not the way you need to hear it, or even worse, how often do you not find it and get sidetracked? (Note: social media marketing can side track you) Do you know where to go to get the answer? Quite frankly, a lot of people might not even bother seeking an answer at all. Yet as we continually head toward more and more computer-based training, there's growing arguments against computers teaching and mentoring folks effectively.

I believe that it's critical for managers to have the ability to train and mentor directly to their employees. The strength of learning that comes from one-on-one human personal connection cannot be overstated.

A huge component of motivating my teams was that when my people struggled, I would show them how and where they were making a mistake or getting tied up – because I knew them personally and how they needed to receive the learning lesson. (A.I. can't do that yet and they won't be able to anytime soon.) I would get in the trenches with my employees so my teams could experience hands-on human to human learning. Then I could look that person in the eye and say, "See how I did that? I know you can, too. I'm right here with you." Your listener's reaction is everything, they are either ready, or need to see and hear it again, often in another way for the learning to stick. Being a good manager is being a good coach.

My aim was to let my teams know they have unlimited creative work ability. I would often say, "The idea that you're not capable is in your mind. The only inability to do the work is in your fear. But once you start and even if you try and fail, try again—you'll get it, and trust me, the fear will go away."

So, leading by example is key. When you can do that, you show that you really understand what's going on and making a connection to your employees too. You can lead as a subject matter expert and are seen as a thought leader. That creates a very upbeat environment, and you can also build an upward spiral of creative thinking.

There are two types of managers. First, there are those who lead by example and are often chosen to be team leaders. These leaders are valued, and they earn the respect of their employees, who believe in them.

On the other-hand, there are managers that lead only because they have a title. They provide neither coaching or support, and often times tell people: "do as I say not as I do." These managers often manage by fear and ultimately do not earn the respect of their employees, who simply do what they are told because they have to.

An upbeat environment brings motivation, inspiration and an innovation spirit. If you are not constantly improving, you're falling behind. Forward movement starts with a positive mindset— learn and train yourself to keep the momentum going. It starts with you.

Active Learning

Keep people involved: Hold quarterly meetings instead of yearly. Select key people who you want to not only attend these meetings but people who you expect to take on a leader role. Identify "team leaders" who will continue to remind others what went on in these meetings. People need to be reminded what's important more than ever; in an information overloaded and a hyper driven world it's easy to forget things. Good leaders are "always-game".

Encourage constant improvement: Look for ways to help educate your team. Implement a mentoring program. Find new tools to help your people succeed. Developing a high performing workforce takes time and continuous energy; you must look at what each person wants individually and help them stay on track to reach their goals.

Keep motivating always: Good managers keep their teams motivated through encouragement, especially when their teams are not performing well. When things aren't working, these managers take the time to create new strategies and talk to their people about their ideas. If something doesn't work in one or two months, they try something else new—they don't let what's not working become the new standard. They are always looking for a better way to do something.

Be mentored: Be a learner and listener for life. Don't let your title and authority get the better of you, that's a sure way to lose. Anyone who thinks they don't need mentoring is wrong. Everyone does. We all need help and support, no one can do it alone. That's why Presidents and CEO's surround themselves with lots of talented people to advise and support them and their goals.

Strategies in Being a Motivating Leader

People skills are critical to leadership and success in anything you do, whether you are leading a club at school, a local soccer team, a theatre group, a non-profit organization, a community association, a small business or a large corporation. The fact that you are reading this book, means you probably think this to be true. Having the skills to illuminate people to your way of thinking without offending them is more important than ever these days, as is being open to other people's ways of thinking and their ideas.

Knowing this is the easy part, while having the skills to persuade as a natural part of your mannerism, is not so easy. Whether you aspire to be a leader, or already are, try these strategies to see how they can benefit you.

Lead by Example

You have heard the phrase "lead by example" and if you are asked to do this, or if you are new in a leader role and you want people to follow your strategy, then it's important to deliver it in a way that folks can replicate your success. By designing a strategy that has worked for you, write down the steps it takes to achieve the repeated success you have attained for replication. This is how you can deliver mentorship. Then, when others follow your example, and they also achieve success, you become what is known as a "subject matter expert or SME". Do this repeatedly and you move into a position of authority with proven expertise.

During my agency career, when candidates came up to visit our offices, I would sometimes see my peers standing around chatting with each other while a candidate stood by the reception desk, in plain sight, while the receptionist was away from her desk. None of them stepped up to meet the candidate. So, I would be the one to go straight to the candidate and say, "Excuse me, is anyone helping you?" I'd help the candidate, and then, I'd walk by my coworkers without saying a word, and get right back to business. That got noticed, because my boss would call me into her office and tell me she appreciated me setting a tone of accountability in around the office. There's a famous quote that states, "Be the change you want to see happen." If you want to lead, or you simply want to see a change happen, you have to "walk the walk" as they say.

Show you care: I had a client, a biotech giant on Wall Street, for whom I was working on a placement deal. It was going to be the first deal we'd done with this company, but at the final step things that were beyond my control, causing the deal to fall through. The client said, "Maybe your firm is not up to the task" and I sensed they were moving the conversation to saying, "Don't call us, we'll call you." I was about to lose the client, if I hadn't already. (To be fair, I inherited the client because of the difficulty of the account. In fact, one of my coworkers literally gave up the account, which no one wanted, so my manager asked me to take it.) But I had built a good rapport with the contact and refused, absolutely refused, to get off the phone until I could apologize in person. After enough pushback from me, my contact conceded and scheduled me to come meet him and apologize face-to-face three week later. I knew my client knew I was located a good two-hours away too, so there was that. As I sat in his office while he wrapped up a call, I saw he had a Philadelphia Eagles helmet on his cabinet. When he hung up the phone, I opened the conversation quickly by telling him I was a Steelers fan and that in World War II the Steelers and the Eagles, due to the draft, formed the Steagles. He was shocked. He googled it immediately. That started a fifty-five-minute conversation of chatting with laughter with nothing about work nor the fallout deal. Finally, with five minutes left my client said, "Look Vinay, I've got a hard stop in five minutes. Send me your top people and let's get you back on the board." I did close that placement deal a month later. What was once a "problem account" became a star business client. Everything changed, and today while he nor I are at the same companies, we are still good friends and networking buddies.

Discuss behaviors: Let's say you have an employee who is sometimes late for meetings by a few minutes. Regardless, the person is always late and it's something you want to change. Before bringing your employee in, think about something minor (but equal weight in your mind to being slightly late) that was once brought to your attention by one of your own past managers. Open by discussing some positive things about your employee's work; in doing this, your goal is to start with praise. Then address the tardy meeting issue and how you'd like to see it change. Immediately go into your story about the past action where you were corrected, and the positive outcome it had with you and your former manager. This kind of open honesty will help your employees know that you are human too, and can make mistakes, and that when an issue was brought to your attention, you corrected your actions and it forged a stronger relationship with your manager. Try this, you might be surprised by the outcome.

Instead of giving orders, give suggestions: In advising subordinates or colleagues or even managing up, instead of saying, "You should do this," or "Don't do that," try making suggestions like, "Have you ever thought of this?" or "I wonder if you tried this what would happen?" This opens a dialogue of ideation. It allows room for the other person to explore their own mistakes. Dale Carnegie wrote, "Giving people options instead of orders makes it easy for a person to correct errors." He went on to say, "A technique like that saves a person's pride and provides him, or her, with a feeling of importance. It encourages cooperation instead of rebellion."

Chapter 4

Work on Your Personal Goals and Dreams

Weight Loss Shines Lessons on Goals

When it comes to weight loss, success stories abound. People who believe they are overweight may join programs like Weight Watchers International, Jenny Craig, and Nutrisystem, every day. The fact is, there's nothing magical about the food these or any other similar organizations sell. These meal program management companies do help people lose weight by teaching them how to set and achieve goals and I believe this is the "secret sauce". That's right; it's about goals and discipline.

This means, fortunately for us, we can apply these same principles to almost any aspect of life that needs improvement – and we can achieve better results.

Choose your goals and dreams—then commit: Meal programs teach us that choice and commitment are the keys to success. Whether you lose weight, attend a class, or put an extra hour in at work, it's all up to you—and your program advocate if you have one, who might be your weight-loss coordinator, or in other instances a teacher, or career coach. That's why people pay for trainers. Once you've chosen and reached a specific goal, you'll feel really good about yourself for accomplishing it! Then, build on that success; go for a new goal and commit to doing it with even more confidence. If you are paying to reach a goal, such as paying for a gym membership, you have "skin in the game," so you will be more likely stick to it and keep building on your success. After a while, achieving goals and success will become more natural and your confidence will continue to build. It's wonderful to be able to look back and see all the successes you are having!

Make sure your goal is reasonable: In weight loss circles, trying to lose 100 pounds in four months isn't a reasonable goal, nor is starting and completing a bachelor's degree in two years. The key is to break down your goal into manageable parts. So, in weight loss parlance, "reasonable" is something like five pounds a month. So is taking a part-time or a full load of classes, but not an overload.

So, for example, if you want to get a degree or even a program certificate to your already busy schedule, start by adding one class per semester to your weekly routine.

Outline your steps for success: The best way to reach your weight-loss goal, or any goal, is to have a concrete plan. At Weight Watchers, they call it storyboarding. This is a plan that shows the steps needed to achieve that "Winning Outcome"—your goal. Each step in your plan inches you ever closer to your goal; you can see it when you put your plan together on paper.

Stay focused on your long-term goal: Visualize your goal. See it in your mind's eye.

Maybe your current goal is to lose weight and your long-term goal is to graduate with a degree. Therefore, you might envision yourself and what you'd look like after losing the weight and walking up to the podium and accepting that diploma. In your mind, see this, practice seeing this—daydream about it.

Once you've lost the weight you will have greater confidence and feel more attractive as you walk down the street. Does that make you smile?

And how much healthier will you feel without carrying those extra pounds around? With that degree, what will you be like sitting in an executive's office interviewing, talking about how you'd like to help his or her company with your new skills? Does this make you happy? I bet it does. Keep daydreaming about it while you work on your goals because it is motivational.

Celebrate victories along the way: Achieving steps along the way to reaching your goal is just as important as the goal itself. At Weight Watchers, they celebrate each five-pound increment of weight loss. When you get that report card and see completed courses with grades, you should celebrate too. Celebration is rewarding; it motivates you to keep the drive alive. It fuels the fire in your spirit to keep going to the finish line.

Ask for and accept help: The most successful weight loss programs have weekly and monthly meetings where participants can gain support, earn praise, and receive one-on-one help with other meeting attendees about their goals, their wins, and how to avoid pitfalls. In the real world, networking and brainstorming with others and attending industry or school functions can help you reach your goals more quickly than going it alone—and it's more fun when you spend time interacting with people about what you want to achieve.

Setting Goals Too High Can Be Dangerous

Did you make a New Year's resolution to start a new exercise or fitness routine? If you did that (as so many of us do), are you looking back at that goal and feeling discouraged or maybe a sense of failure? Don't beat yourself up just yet.

Truth is, a lot of us set up goals that we really want to reach, but we set ourselves up for failure. Many fitness and health experts say most people who decide to start a new exercise program set goals too high. Folks decide to start running at the gym every day for the next six months as a big goal or don't set any goals and just buy a membership.

The key to meeting any goal is to properly prepare for what that goal looks like and how you are going to achieve it. After all, you have to remember that reaching any goal doesn't happen overnight. First you must decide on your goal. Decreasing your risk of having a heart attack can be a goal. Maybe making more sales calls? Want to lose weight? Get a more muscular physique? Do you want to join a weekend softball team but convinced yourself you will when you're in better shape?

After you've decided what you would most like to achieve, it's very important to figure out how much time you can really devote to your goal. The key is to be realistic. If you are working two jobs and want to devote enough time in the gym to lose ten pounds in the next three months, you have to be honest with yourself. You need to properly align your goal and your ability to commit to making it happen.

If you realize they don't align, it's not the end of the world. Whatever you do don't give up. That's where so many people fail, or stop trying. It's the *All or Nothing Syndrome*. Instead, adjust to a smaller goal so you can achieve and start building toward the larger goal.

If weight loss is the goal, regardless of the level at which you set your goal, and yes, even if you do a small goal, will be burning calories and fat as opposed to doing nothing. So, for example, start meeting your goals slowly by adding a little time at the gym – or even the office.

Tips to Get You Started

- Stand up when you are talking to clients at work or in your social group setting. Standing up and even moving around will give you more energy. Walking and talking can even help some folks focus more than when sitting in a recliner. Many people use Bluetooth headsets too.

- Do light exercises like sit-ups, squats, or air jump rope at home when watching TV. If you want to concentrate on what you're watching, then exercise during the commercials. Getting in even a little fitness time is better than nothing and it helps to get your body and mind in sync so you can achieve your goals.
- Wear your gym shoes to the mall or grocery shopping and try walking in step when you stop in the aisles too. Remember, any walking is exercise, plus it's simple and costs nothing.

I remember reading about former President Barak Obama and his walks along the West Wing to get-to-and-from the Oval Office. When I read about his short one-or two-minute open-air commutes, which he would often make several times a day, I remember that he explained how it provided a way for him to gather his thoughts for the day while he prepared for conversations with members of The House and Senate. He would think about his plans and proposals to move the country forward. That stuck with me, and I figured if the president could do one-minute walks I could take a minute to walk from office-to-office to gather my own thoughts about moving forward in my own life. When I'm at work I switch out of my dress shoes and into my walking shoes and I make an effort to get up and walk over to colleagues who are close by instead of sitting in my cubical e-mailing and texting folks all day. I might be getting up and walking 10 or 15 times a day. It's a little extra exercise, plus it provides a more humanistic way to communicate with people in your office. You see people, you can smile, have a moment of conversation about something, even the weather. It's a way of connecting with other people and breaking up the stress on the eyes from staring at your computer monitor for hours too.

Make more walking a conscious goal every day. Something else I did was sell the idea of "brainstorming" to a colleague and walking around the office after eating during our lunch time, rather than sitting in at our office desks, eating lunch and surfing the internet. If you are working from home, take a walk and get some fresh air.

If taking short walks to clear your head and strategize works for presidents of the United States it can work for you.

Want a Better Version of You? Learn to create and Stay Focused on Goals

Are you good at goal-setting but wonder why you struggle to accomplish your goals? Don't be discouraged; you are not alone. Believe it or not, your own creativity could be the problem.

Many researchers have found that creative or "right-brain dominated" people tend to generate ideas and goals and want to pursue all of them at the same time. What is the downside? They end up starting many projects, partially finishing all of them, but completing few to none.

If this sounds like you, don't worry—many of us have the same problem. Guess what - Thomas Edison, Ben Franklin, and Albert Einstein are just a few of the many famous creative people who are just like you.

The trick is that we have to be strategic when it comes to setting goals. To do that the left and right sides of our brains need to work together in setting and achieving your goals:

Dream about your goals: Take some time and really think about what you want for yourself. What does the perfect job look like? Or imagine yourself in front of your home in five years. What does that look like? If you had all the money in the world, what would you be doing with it? Write these dreams down—you've got to capture it.

Choose your first goal: First, you want to focus on one goal and really give it a solid effort. Keep the other goals on your list as motivation, because you should know that when you finish the current goal, you get to move onto the next one.

Scrutinize yourself: Many researchers suggest that you record the way you spent the last week, hour by hour. You know, kind of like counting steps or calories. Categorize your hours into sleeping, eating, shopping, exercise, cleaning, surfing the web, consuming social media, visiting friends, playing Xbox (if you do that), and working — obviously, create a list that works for you.

Goal success equals controlling time: You must take a hard look and calculate how many hours you are doing things that move you closer to your real goal. Just as important in this exercise is, calculate how many hours or activities are retracting you from reaching your goal. If you want to lose thirty pounds but spend more hours sitting on the couch watching TV and very little time doing exercises or being active and mobile, there is a good chance you're not going to reach your goal of losing weight. But the best part about this process is that it's your choice and you can make change. Time is finite; you must control every minute of it. When you start doing this and seeing it on paper, you'll be amazed at what you can control your time and thrilled you are finally doing this (you might kick yourself for not having started this a long time ago!) This is critical for goal success.

Weigh the importance of your activities: Put your activities on a scale of 1 through 5, from most important to least important. Ranking your activities will help you see the ones that matter to you.

· ·

The Critical Core Four

- *Get started immediately.* Do not put your goal off for another week or month.
- *Beware of what you "think" is important.* Interruptions abound in our daily lives, like social media or feeling the need to respond to someone right away. Researchers acknowledge this and suggest, "Just because something is in front of you does

not mean you're required to respond to it." Do the best you can to control your own time and not be ruled by sudden or unexpected interruptions.

- *Each week, review how you are doing.* How can you tinker or adjust yourself to get a little better at reaching your goal? Work on this.
- *Celebrate the little achievements.* Set little milestones and reward yourself. Take a moment and congratulate yourself. Realize you are getting closer to your goal and that you did accomplish something instead of having not started. Look back and be proud you are not at the starting line.

How to Make Your Goals Come True

I am a first-generation American. My Dad was born by the famous Ganges River, but there's a different level of poverty for many people living near the river too. It's hard for many Americans to imagine. Growing up, I visited the Ganges River region a few times. When I returned in 1999, after more than a two decades away, and saw the way folks were living I thought, "These people in this village can't possibly conceptualize what I take for granted. And because my dad studied so hard to get out of this village, I get to take a lot of things for granted."

When I was young, I asked my mom how we got to this country. She said, "Your Dad was the number-one engineering student in the land. That's how he got a scholarship to M.I.T. After I married your dad, they (M.I.T.) came and said, 'Son, pack your bags. You're coming with us.'" When I got older, I thought, I'm pretty sure they didn't actually say that, but I knew my dad had been dead set on getting out of the village and accomplishing big things. I was sure my dad visualized himself getting out.

He used to always tell me: "You can accomplish anything if you put your mind to – if you are willing to do the hard work - but do it now—

because tomorrow never comes." Honestly, I hated hearing that—yet I heard it all the time! So, at a young age I was a goal-setter and imagined what I'd like to accomplish.

By the time I reached college, I would visualize my goals in my mind. When I was growing up, parents and teachers always told us kids to stop daydreaming. It wasn't encouraged. Today it's called visualization and while it is encouraged it's not talked about nearly as often in the mainstream as it should be. Early in my career I often visualized how I wanted meetings to go and I'd even role play in my head how I wanted the conversations to go.

I remember reading about Olympic gold medal winning snowboarder Shaun White who said that visualization was something that he did for goal setting. He might be sitting on an airplane waiting to take off, visualizing what his next competitive event would be like. He would visualize what he would be wearing, visualize his competitors, as well as the course in front of him, picturing himself in the event, and so forth.

While my visualization was not quite as exciting as competing in the Olympics, it did help me get through my day more smoothly. I would visualize my commute to a meeting or presentation, entering a prestigious Manhattan office building, then sitting across from several high- level executives in a well-decorated office overlooking the city. I could even visualize the suit I would be wearing and the matching tie. Visualization is painting a picture of what you see ahead of you so when you experience it, you know what to expect. Familiarity breeds comfort, and when we visualize our surroundings, we become more familiar with the environment and more comfortable and confident.

I also found it interesting that Shaun White mentioned that when he was 14 or 15, when he used to visualize being able to drive. I'm sure this is familiar to many teenagers, picturing themselves in the car, starting the engine and driving off. For Shawn it was a bit different – he would visualize the cars he would win in events, and then when he won, he'd give the car away to other people with licenses.

The truth is you don't have to be an inventor or athlete to achieve your goals, no matter how far away they seem. You just have to know what you want and continue to visualize doing what you need to do to reach that goal.

. . . .

Getting Started

Take time to meditate:
A well-known Hindu priest explains that meditation in its simplest form is intentional thinking. I agree with that. When you meditate you and your mind are able to become very aware and mindful of your thoughts, without silencing of them.

As a long-time *Star Wars* fan, I think Yoda is awesome, I like the fact that whenever a Jedi would approach him with a problem, Yoda would say, "Meditate on this I will," and he would meditate and direct his thoughts to solving the problem at hand.

Meditation is a form of reflective thinking. Some developmentally reflective processes are critical to a person advancing not just spiritually, but in their careers, and in their other endeavors. Reflective thinking such as meditation is a marvelous way of countering the hyper pace of our world today with the wisdom of age-old scholars, and philosophers. The benefits of mindfulness come from this.

Reflect on your greatest accomplishment (even if you haven't reached it yet)
While the following suggestion may seem ridiculous or pointless: think about being on your deathbed, what would it be that you would say that you accomplished?

Write it down: Study after study shows that writing down your goals increases your chances of achieving them.

Focus on your goals and then break them into smaller, achievable milestones. For example, if your goal is to build an extension on your home, you break the process into stages: creating a budget and saving for each stage while you talk to contractors and get estimates. You'll be doing this while you visualize what goes into the new addition, like the paint and the furnishings. Or maybe you want to write a book. Start by focusing on what you want to write about, possible titles and what you'll include in each of the chapters. Create the outline first. You can visualize these things before you even start writing.

The point is, what appears to be a monumental goal becomes much more manageable with mini goals that will lead you to achieve the success you want.

Focus on your "End Goal."
And finally, it's important to focus on the outcome, but do not fixate more on the results than on the job itself. What I mean is, don't lose sight of the process of getting the job done. Often focusing on the end result takes you away from the importance of each step you need to get there. Remember, celebrate benchmarks, and small successes, as you strive for each important step.

Get focused and organized: Buy a new notebook and organizer. Write down your to-do lists and all the data that comes with trying to accomplish the tasks in those lists. Keep a record of people, events, and motivational articles, anything that will help you reach your goals.

The key to achieving your goal is to keep it always "alive", and within your reach. Using visualization and good record keeping of your mini goal achievements will allow you to realize the big goals you set out to accomplish.

Time for spring cleaning—Start with your brain

Each new year is full of big possibilities; so, it's time to dust off that list of goals from last year. Goals, just like life, are not static. As you change, so should your goals.

Whatever the season is as you are reading this book, take time to really reflect on what you want to accomplish and get out of life—but especially what you want to accomplish this year. Unlike writing down your goals on a piece of paper and forgetting about them, make a new practice of reviewing your goals regularly to adjust them as you adjust to your life's changes. We are living in a very volatile time, one of the most volatile times in modern history and because we are in the beginning of the first truly global push for a work-from-anywhere society. It's a hyper speed and disruptive economy to say the least. In making your goals, consider: "Every day is a new day. I'm going to get up every day with my mind set on improving something. I need to be fluid and flexible—it's a hyper economy, and it's okay for me to pivot and tweak my goals, I don't need to be rigid."

If your goals seem too distant and you don't think you can reach them, then I suggest trying this new activity. Do research on your favorite famous people. Chances are you'll come up with one who came from real hardship, beyond anything you've got going on in your life. For me, it was the actor, Sidney Poitier. He was born to a poor family, yet by age sixteen he had paid his own way to New York City. He wanted to be an actor; the problem was that he read so poorly he could not read for the auditions. So, Sidney got a job as a dishwasher, saved for a radio, and listened to broadcasts constantly. Eventually he saved enough for acting classes. He made incremental adjustments to reach his goals. And you can too.

Adjusting Your Goals to Fit the New Version of You:

Take a look at your goals. How do you feel about them today?

- Are your goals still what you're looking to do? Are you willing to tweak them and work really hard to achieve them?
- What stopped you from fulfilling your goals last time? Is that going to happen again?
- Is a roadblock stopping you from reaching your goal? Can you do something to prevent that roadblock?

Do you need to focus on achieving a few smaller goals this year to reach your ultimate goal?

The bottom line is if you really want to succeed at your goals, you can. It may take adjusting and even realizing you've got to overcome a few things — those are also goals—but you can do it if you really are 100 percent committed.

Make a mental note: To stay flexible in your goals, modify your goals as your life's routine changes – just don't give up on them.

Goals Are the Framework for Career Success

Who doesn't have goals? On the surface, every time you think or say: "I really want" or "It would be really great if" well guess what? You have a desire, or a wish to set goals. The key is to use these desires and thoughts to propel you to act.

Here is a real-life example of having a goal and sticking to it for a very long time.

When I was in high school, like many teens, I wanted to attend an Ivy League school. But my grades were bad in high school, so I knew I wasn't getting in. Yet I believed I belonged there. Well, because my grades were bad, I was only accepted to two small universities and attended one of them that was only a few hours from my parents' home. I got my grades up, so I could transfer to The Ohio State University—a major upgrade! Once there, I enjoyed myself way too much, but I had conquered social anxieties that plagued me during high school. I took advantage of fraternity living. Eventually, I graduated with a GPA only David Letterman and John Blutarsky would be proud of. When I got into the workforce, I started very well, but in my fifth year of working, the dot-com crash came. Shortly after, the 9-11 tragedy hit my local area of New York, and the first company at which I worked went through stages of layoffs and eventually went out of business. At that point, I decided to pursue a Master's degree at a good technical school. It was tough, but the timing was right. With the added five years of experience working with corporate executives, I started an MBA at New Jersey Institute of Technology (NJIT). This time, I thought, there would be no hanky-panky. Two years later and I graduated on time with a 3.3 GPA. I believed that the GPA was still not good enough for Ivy League. A few years later I moved to Manhattan and this time it was during the Great Recession, so I felt the need to reskill again. I decided to do a graduate diploma at New York University with my focus on ensuring the GPA was at minimum a 3.5, and I got that two years later. Then, right when the covid pandemic hit, I applied and got accepted to Columbia University for my second Master's degree, and in 2021 I finished with a GPA high of 3.9. It took me more than 25 years after graduating high school, but I always knew I could get in. And I did. I achieved an important goal in my life.

The moral of the story is that you must be your own champion. After all, who will support your ideas and believe in you if you don't? So, it's important that you commit yourself to your goals – short term and long term. Whatever it is, learning to cook Italian cuisine, saving a million dollars, traveling to all the wonders of the world, or getting into a great school, stick to your goals and keep plugging away, and don't give up. Commit to it and you shall have it.

Here are some ideas that can help you get started:

Choose one goal to pursue immediately: Your immediate goal should be something that can help you get toward one of your ultimate goals. For example, let's say you want to save a million dollars. To do so, you feel you need to be making more money. Earning more money could involve getting a degree that you don't have. So, your immediate goal is to enroll in that degree and start right away with one class.

Choose successful mentors: Have someone you can turn to for emotional support, advice, financial assistance, and other expertise's. Comedian Jay Leno gained his confidence because even in detention, during high school, teachers laughed at his stories. Having the right people around you will help tremendously—for example, it's been said that Steve Martin saw Leno's skit on stage and got him an appearance on "The Tonight Show" with Johnny Carson. Even great inventors like Thomas Edison, *who never appeared on "The Tonight Show,"* had a lot of bright people around him all the time to help fuel his great inventions.

The question is: how can you do this? It could start with thinking outside the box and getting active and involved in things you might not normally do. For example, ask to meet with managers one-on-one in departments at your company, that are adjacent to yours and learn about what they do. Then tell them about your interests in that department, and even ask how you may be of help to their team. If you aren't comfortable talking to managers in other departments, ask peers to meet you for lunch and learn from them. Grow your network that way. Build on your interests by joining after-work groups that are work-related or non-work related. LinkedIn, Facebook and Meetup.com offer endless possibilities for you to experience new groups and build new network and friendships that can take you down a whole host of roads. This isn't only for people in corporate America, but for people in any type of business or industry anywhere in the world. Network and learn.

Always keep believing: We've all heard: "When the going gets tough, the tough get going." You've got to be that. Find stories of people you admire who have overcome great obstacles– then keep them around so you can always reference them. Abraham Lincoln endured the deaths of his mother, sister, and his three young sons. It's been written that he failed at business and had a nervous breakdown. In politics, we know him as a President, but did you know he was defeated as a candidate for Congress in 1843 and in 1844? Then he was defeated as a candidate for the Senate in 1855 and then defeated as a vice presidential candidate in 1856? Lincoln wanted to be President; he fought for everything he believed in—and he finally succeeded. Then he set out to defy conventional thinking and make our nation see a vision of civil equality.

Write down steps you can take toward reaching your goal: Ask yourself some hard questions to see what it will take to get you to where you want to be:

- You may have to give up some activities to make your goals come true—what are they – (be honest)?
- Is your goal worth giving up the things you've written down?
- What is your current financial situation?
- What can you do to change your financial situation?
- What is the time line in which you want to achieve your goal?
- What kind of toll will this put on the people closest to you?
- Can you handle it from an emotional standpoint?

Chapter 5

Making Your Career Goals Come True

Making Your Dreams a Reality

At my first job, a private company, the president had a kind of "rock-star status". It was widely understood that he was friends with Bill Parcells, head coach of the New York Giants, and other folks like world famous musicians. At every Annual New Year meeting, he would tell us about his struggles and someone who was willing to do whatever it took to succeed. He explained how he worked really hard to build the multi-branch staffing conglomerate which was the company I worked at. It reminded me of my own father's story of getting out of a village in India and how he literally walked to the city center to study under the lights because there was no electricity in the village. He did that and I remember visiting that village several times as a young pre-teenager, so that stuck with me.

My Dad and the president of my company were both role models for me that went the extra mile, so to speak. I learned from them to do what others were not willing to do. I worked about three or four hours every Saturday and Sunday in the mornings for the first five years of my career. When I became a manager, I asked my teams to come in on the weekends to get ahead, but it was not mandatory. Most people didn't come in at first. But many times, my subordinates asked me how I was such a high producer and how they could achieve my results. I told them, "I'm willing to do what others won't do and even do what is uncomfortable – like coming in on the weekends. This prepares me to not just be able to hit the ground running on Monday, but to get way ahead. So, while everyone else is picking up work where they left off on Friday, I'm already way ahead of them and that's why I'm consistently one of the top producers every month." Over time, I saw more and more of my subordinates coming in on weekends looking to achieve higher levels of success because they did have the desire to achieve more, but previously, no one who told them how to.

How does this relate to making your dreams come true you may be asking? It's all about self-engagement – if you engage yourself in what you do, and leave the distractions aside, (like drama at work), you will begin to enjoy what you are doing and then you could start to feel more motivated in your career... and in life overall.

Find a dream you want to make a reality: Start by asking yourself if you have what it takes to make your dreams come true. Have you thought about this? Ask yourself some hard questions like, "Would I be doing what I'm doing if I wasn't making enough money to meet my financial goals?" Sometimes this is tricky, and you really have to put some thought into it.

Ask yourself these questions:
What do I like to do?
If you think about yourself doing your dream job, what are you doing? Are there certain industries you wish you were in -but you are not working in there yet?

Identifying whether your dreams are real or pipedreams: Can you reach your dreams; are they a realistic goal? To see if your dream is something you can achieve cross check it with your real values in life and see what you come up with.

Write down the things you like to do professionally and personally.

- Think of your life and put down your greatest accomplishments.
- Write down the things you love to do but don't get time to do anymore.
- What is the core of who you are? For example, are you a motivator, a teacher, a follower, a cheerleader?
- What are the core values and qualities that you want to exude or express?

If you take some time to contemplate and write down your answers, you'll start to see things that are meaningful to you. A common theme should emerge and this is the essence of your goal and true dream.

Even if you don't see how this can translate into something that you can do today, keep talking to people in your circles and network. Focus your efforts on your goals and dreams, and you will find the path that leads you to true happiness…. but remember, sometimes things take more time than you anticipate – that's okay, as they say "good things come to those who wait."

Change Your Thinking: Shift from focusing on adversity to focusing on motivation and achieving your goals.

Think about the adversity you have faced. Do you look at adversity and throw your hands up in the air with the belief that there is nothing you can do about the challenges that you face or do you think about how you can succeed despite the adversity around you? Facing and overcoming adversity can help you in your adult life just like any form of education.

Here's a true story: During the dot-com days, my manager landed an introductory meeting with a senior leader of a top technology storage company. This company hired hard-core techies in "Wall Street" suits; and they were top-level professional services experts. As we sat in this man's office, he leaned back and said, "You're a minute late". PS - we were not. Next, looking at my boss, he said, "Don't send me any women. I'm not hiring skirts." Then he looked at me and said, "Don't send me anyone who looks like you." Now, I must tell you, we could easily have gotten up and walked out, we could have told this person we were very offended and had every right to be – the guy just discriminated against women and minorities! But we didn't leave.

Forty-five minutes later we did walk out, with our firm signed onto their vendor list and a big promise by me personally that I'd surpass their other vendor firm's capabilities by producing the best candidates and giving their company the best service, they would ever experience. As we walked out of the building my boss said the account was mine. My personal goal was to find a way to turn the tide and get this client to hire the best candidate, including if it was a woman or a person of color. That said, it was an account like nothing else we had worked with previously; I had to find real business professionals that were technical folks too, and this was before the dot com crash. Back then, we were working with all kinds of start-up dot coms and techies wore ripped jeans and Star Wars t-shirts! Other technical folks looked like everyday folks, but this companies wanted the "wall street look". I took this account on and worked very hard. I was relentless in my creativity to break though the admin and the technical support layers of companies. Often times these groups of folks were screening for recruiters, making sure we didn't get past them to the technical folks. You have to remember, there was no social media so recruiting was quite a different challenge!

Within two years, I had placed so many folks at this client that all my candidates became hiring managers in New Jersey, New York City, and eastern Pennsylvania. I had excellent relationships with all of them, and for obvious reasons, they had high respect for me since I placed them. The corporate HR office - located many states away - would politely request I keep them posted on the hiring managers' plans and the newest forecasted job requests I would be working on because I knew more than they did about the company's hiring needs in the tri-state area. By that time, my staffing firm had expanded from four to six branches. Everyone across the branches knew about this account too: if anyone wanted to place their candidate at this hyper-growing storage company, there was only one person in the greater New York area that could make that happen - me.

My motivation and dedication to overcome and look past adversity in the beginning made me widely respected within my company at all levels. Also, two years in, I had all but eliminated my vendor competition too. Guess what? By the time I established my staffing firm and really, myself as the "go-to" northeast recruiter for this company, I was placing women and minorities there as well. Did I accomplish my goal? You bet.

I put a personal feeling away, it didn't matter that this hiring manager insulted me – after all, what if it was some kind of "test"? Was I going to let his words, which I genuinely felt were a tactic to see if I had thick skin, ruin my chances of doing amazing work and generating a lot of compensation for myself and my firm? Nope. As you read this example, it was a different time period too. But, my point is not for you to accept inconsiderate people, but rather, my goal here is for you to see how my boss and I weighed our goals, and took a little "on the chin" so as to gain rewards that far outweighed that remark.

Be inspired, not intimidated, by people who say, "can't do:" For the years I plugged away with this corporate client, one of many in my portfolio, but many people told me I would not be able to handle this high-level, hard-core, type-A personality, demanding client. The more I heard, "don't bother, you can't" the more I was fueled to "bother, I can and will."

Live your convictions: Most of my life I've been told I couldn't do, and that goes back to my high school days when I had poor grades. I dealt with a ton of social issues, that in 2022, wouldn't even be thinkable, which weighed on me getting poor grades. That didn't stop me from attaining an Ivy league degree. In the example above, I worked more hours than I did on any other account, and I ended up placing women and people who looked just like me.

Believe in yourself: Focus on building your inner strength and high self-esteem. If you develop a belief that you can reach your goals you can.

Oftentimes, it will not be easy, and set back can abound, but you "belief in self" can be your most powerful ally.

Throughout history we see inspiring stories of people who overcame adversity time and again. You can, too.

Goal Setting Can Help You Soar!

I think everyone can benefit from spending time working in a form of business development or sales capacity. Working in sales and having to hustle gives people a great perspective of what it's like to hustle, make ends meet with the kind of compensation structure that comes with these roles and also what it's like to perform good customer and advisory service. When you move out of sales, it also gives you a lasting appreciation for what full scope salesmanship is. A huge benefit to working in sales is that you learn to set performance goals, but unlike non sales positions, if you miss your performance goals, there are consequences that can range from not getting the compensation you were expecting to eventually being let go and having to learn life lessons like how to be resilient. Sales roles can be serious positions that demand your absolute best – and your goals are usually tied to a person's performance per month, so there's no time to sit around, and that in itself is a worthy lesson in life. Setting goals is a positive management technique that most sales roles incorporate and the training in goal setting that comes from these jobs makes achieving milestones and deadlines a priority.

Having spent more than ten years in a quota-sales environment, and competing for monthly top producer statuses, gave me a solid foundation in project management, revenue generation and client development. The experiences has helped me understand the importance of timelines and builds an understanding for things like sense of urgency, client expectations, outside the box thinking, time management and setting expectations. After some time spent in this capacity, when I achieved my monthly goals, I didn't default to "relax mode." I built a foundation to keep achieving. That came from consistently working to achieve monthly short-term goals and keeping my eye on the ball for the overall quarterly and yearly target goals.

Setting goals does not have to be a hard thing to do. Start by thinking about what you have to achieve and in what time frame. Whatever it is, write it down; make it a journal or keep it on your iPad, so you can refer back to it because as developments happen, your goals need adjustments and you want to stay flexible and fluid with your planning.

Write down your goals for your future: When you write it down you start the practice of making the goal concrete, now it's something you have envisioned for yourself but can see it. Aim high. By aiming high, you motivate yourself.

When writing goals, be specific: As you write goals, be sure to add specifics about what you want to achieve. For example, don't just write, "I want a million dollars." Being specific would mean writing, "I want to earn a million dollars by the time I reach my 40th birthday." Now you've given yourself a direction for jump-starting your goal but adding sub-goals for example, if you are age 30, you have 10 years to get there. What will you do for each of your ten yearly goals to ensure you get to your overall target goal? You are now developing a comprehensive goal strategy and building time management in as well.

Make your goals just that— yours: You will succeed if you create your goals for yourself, not someone else. In other words, make these goals personal achievements that you want – "you want to go to college because you want to achieve _____, not you want to go to college because your parents want you to go."

Being positive is a key to success: Instead of writing down a goal like, "I wish I had more dates," write something more positive like, "I now choose to go out more and make new friends." Studies have shown that "your mind moves you toward whatever you think about."

Don't use "lack of talent" as an excuse. So many of the "greats" failed somewhere along the line. For example, Michael Jordan was cut from his high school basketball team. What separates the winners from the pack is that they have a "never give up" attitude—that's what you need to adopt to win. Try a range of things that interest you is also important. Just because you're not good at something, doesn't mean you can't learn it - or excel at something else. Find what you are passionate about and ask yourself honestly: Do I really have what it takes to be great at this? For example, I know that being 5'6", no matter how much I learned or practiced, it was extremely unlikely that I could ever be a great basketball player – I had no delusions! That being said, I knew I was really good at debating, understanding enterprise technologies and working with all kinds of people. So, I became a top producer and then a managing director of a technology staffing firm.

Make a list of small steps: Make a list of small steps to inch your way towards whatever your goals are. If a step seems too big, them break that one into two smaller steps. For example, if you want to save $300 dollars, start by eating out one less night a month, and then consider making taking your lunch from home to work.

Say yes to new and no to old habits: Be strong and start using your time more wisely toward achieving your new goals. Start to eliminate old habits that are useless to you, for example, like watching late night television. Some of reading this might think "no way, I can't do that!" Challenge yourself: shave off just 30 minutes at night and get up 30 minutes earlier. See what happens for 30 days. Now, if you start to see how another 30 minutes of late night TV equals getting to work early, studying an online course or adding an hour of exercise in the morning before going to work does indeed benefit your life, you might realize huge benefits and be amazed.

CEO's Choose "Stretch Goals" and You Can Too

One way to be successful is set some impossible goals. That's what General Electric Co.'s (GE) Jack Welch did, and it worked for him. Welch, the late GE Chief Executive, called the tough targets he set for himself and his company "stretch goals."

"We've set these goals and either reached them or came close," Welch told GE shareholders in April 1997. "But even in missing them, we delivered performance greater than we ever thought was in us." Setting lofty goals leads to ambitious thinking, Welch asserts.

Heads of the nation's top-performing, publicly traded companies polled by top surveys agree. About 97 percent say their goal orientation is high or very high and 92 percent frequently or almost always achieve the goals they've set.

Goals can help you to:

Gain momentum: Welch believed that while reaching for goals, you become more energetic and achieve greater things than you thought possible. By the time you achieve your goal, you'll raise your own hopes and increase your skills.

Create focus: Once you've set goals, refine them, and focus on them— to the exclusion of almost everything else.

Bounce back: If I had allowed the poor grades I got back in high school and undergrad let me think I would never get into an Ivy League school, I would have never attempted to keep trying. Because I set that goal, I have two masters' degrees and at Columbia University I was so focused on achieving excellence, I achieved all A's and only one B+.

Here's another example: A man named Fred Smith, once got a poor grade on his college paper about his idea of an express delivery service. He wrote the idea "for a nationwide delivery company that specialized in time-sensitive goods." The paper got a C, but that didn't slow down Smith. He believed in his goal and stuck with it. He is the founder and Chief Executive of Federal Express, better known as FedEx.

Smith went ahead and bought an aviation service in the late sixties and ordered two studies on the concept of overnight delivery. When the studies supported his idea, Smith worked night and day to achieve his goal. He raised money and launched his company in 1971. The company almost went under several times but he stuck with it.

The company turned its first profit in 1976. Today FedEx is a leader in the business it invented, express shipping, and had a net worth of 73.4 billion dollars as of 12/2020. Not bad, eh? You can do this too.

Chapter 6

Learn to Take Action and Build a Winning Mentality

Procrastinating Stops Now!

We are all human; and yes, we put things off. However, we don't have to. Successful people practice the art of taking immediate action. President Franklin D. Roosevelt, who was famous for not procrastinating, said "Take a method and try it. If it fails, try another."

Taking action sounds easy, right? It's not. Most of us inadvertently, pick up both good and bad habits from our parents. As kids, we have a voracious appetite for learning, copying, and remembering what we see our parents do. So, when we would see our parents putting things off or saying things like "not right now, I'll do it later" we get the idea that it's okay to procrastinate. So, what eventually happens is kids turn into teenagers who take this reasoning with them when they go off to college. They avoid studying for tests until the last minute. Do you remember pulling all-nighters, studying with friends in the dorm? If you're honest, I'm sure you're thinking, "Yes, all too well. If I could go back now, I would have done that differently."

Most of us didn't really understand what it meant when our parents would say, "Do as I say, not as I do" until we were grown up.

This is one of the reasons many of us have chronic organizational problems or have built-in procrastination habits. If you are ready to be honest with yourself, you can start to reverse procrastination. But, to do so you need to ask yourself some questions:

Developmental: Do I often avoid tasks that make me feel uncomfortable or stressed? Do I put off deadlines? Do I find myself racing to make deadlines at the last minute? Have I bought into the philosophy that "you work better under pressure?"

Routine: Do I handle responsibilities efficiently at work, but my home is a mess with bills piling up?

Do I tell myself that since I'm organized at work, it's okay to have a messy home?

Health: Having health problems are tough for all of us. But putting them off and thinking that work or other things are more important can be a big mistake. Nothing should be more important to you than your health.

Missed Opportunity: You planned on going through the jobs you want to apply for on Sunday morning but your friends call and you go to brunch with them instead. Other things pop up on that Sunday morning, and now you are deterred from even bothering to do that positive action item. You convince yourself you're fine and happy. A few months later you read about someone in your industry who just got the dream job at a company where you really wish you could work. Do you wonder, "Was that the job I could have applied for that Sunday?"

Telling yourself life is just getting in the way, and finding excuses on a regular basis result in a habit of procrastinating. After all, it's much easier to do nothing.

What can you do? How do you reverse this cycle of procrastination? Good news: there are small, easy steps to break the procrastination habits.

Play to your strengths and develop your weaknesses

Understand where your problems areas are. Accept that you can't be the best at everything, nobody can be great at everything they do – we all have strengths and weaknesses. Combat your weakness by playing to your strengths and play them up, while also working to get better in your weak areas instead of settling for "that's just how it is." There are so many classes you can take today - and books you can read or listen to – so you can improve in any area of your life if you really want to.

Learn to feel discomfort as proactive self-training: Train your mind to acknowledge that the uncomfortable feeling of starting something right now instead of putting it off is why you will succeed in your long-term goals. As President John F. Kennedy said, "There are always risks and costs to a program of action —but they are far less than the long-range risk of comfortable inaction."

Choose bite-sized tasks: Whatever task you want to do, start small by doing a little at a time. This will build your momentum into doing it a little longer. For example, if you want to learn another language, start listening to lessons for one hour a week, then watch how you pick up steam and are doing this a few hours a week.

Try the ten percent rule: Whatever it is you're trying to achieve; the following week add ten percent more and do the same of whatever that is the week after. If this works, try adding another ten percent and see if you are even more productive than you were last week. For example, if it's the exercise, try walking ten percent more than you were before. Keep working from that point. In time you will find a more productive rate.

It's been said that being ten percent better than the next guy is the only thing separating superstar athletes from the rest of the pack.

Famous Motivator and Speaker Denis Waitley said, "Only five percent of salespeople keep calling after the tenth try." Guess what? They are the superstars.

The Trick to Business Success is Being Action-Oriented

Many surveys show leaders of top-performing businesses look for action-oriented workers. But 46 percent of the executives either delegate or procrastinate when faced with an uncomfortable task, according to media polls. In those polls, when executives were asked what they do when faced with an unpleasant job—delegate, procrastinate, or immediately do it themselves, the stats are revealing: 49 percent said they do the task themselves, 37 percent procrastinate, 9 percent delegate, and 5 percent had no response.

Just like we follow our parent's examples when we are children, we also follow the lead when the boss and other executives pass the buck or avoid jobs, and since this is the case, it's clear that hiring action-oriented workers isn't enough. The initiative starts with leadership and flows downward. If you've got top performers with a manager who delegates and isn't action-oriented, eventually that will infect the whole group. A strong manager will convey expectations through positive action in everything they do. You can see the impact right away because people start doing things and things get done.

Saving money – start early: One area in which people tend to procrastinate, rather than taking action, is saving money for your future. The trick is to start putting money away when you're young, as soon as you can afford to so someday you can enjoy retirement. This way you won't have to work so hard when you get older. Unfortunately, the uncomfortable truth is that most of us get sidetracked with our spending mannerisms and put little to nothing away year after year and before you know it, decade after decade. Far too many of us come to realize in later stages of life that we've got nowhere near enough to retire and are left with an unexpected reality of having to adjust our retirement goals or even working for as long as possible.

I acknowledge that saving money is not easy, especially if you aren't making very much. However, if possible, it's important to save even a little bit early on so it builds that continuous momentum of an investment nest egg, which according to most data, demands diligent saving if a person is to achieve a strong and solid nest egg. Often, it's just forcing yourself to skip a few little things that you pay for each week. But, it can pay off.

For example, according to Motley Fool, if you put away $10 a week starting with some of your allowance or earnings at part time jobs, when you were 15 years old, by the time you reached 60, you could have $165,776. At $20 a week you could have $331,553. And if you started a little later on when you could afford $50 per week at the age of 22, you could have $828,882 by age 67.

If you ignore saving money when you're young, you could be playing catch up for life.

Get Down to Business and Focusing to Win

I want to tell you about a man named James Murphy. He flew missions in the Middle East, among other places, while he was a pilot in the Air Force and Air National Guard. After his career as a pilot, he became a sales manager for a national paint company and ended up boosting the annual revenues up from five million to over fifty million in two years. That is some serious increase in productivity.

James Murphy took action; and he wrote about his success. He translated what he learned as a fighter pilot to business in his book *Business Is Combat*. Murphy wrote: "The discipline. The planning. The attitude. The process that turned me and thousands of other people into fighter pilots was nothing short of a textbook for the creation of cutting-edge business warriors." That's good stuff.

James made the correlation between air combat and business combat, which he taught to clients at IBM, Dell, and Home Depot through his management training company, Afterburner Seminars.

In almost any type of business, you can find correlations. In other words, what works for one type of business or activity can also work for another. However, maintaining a winning attitude is tough in today's demanding world. Here are some tips to keep you focused and on the ball:

One thing at a time: Focus on the job at hand. Put yourself "in the moment and focus on what you have to accomplish right now." You can't listen to a speaker presentation and get 100 percent out of it while you are busy texting. Listening for ideation generation is much more effective if you're not being distracted.

Less talk, listen more: Brevity is the soul of business speak, suggests James Murphy, and I agree. Murphy says it well: "A few well-chosen words can close a business deal, clear the air in a conflict or communicate a vision to employees." As it is, most of us spend too much time in meetings. Try to keep your meetings short but to the point, and achieve what you need to by end the session. Have an agenda and stick to it. You'll be more productive—also try doing it with memos and emails too. Get to the point quickly and concisely.

Practice and prepare: When dealing with clients or customers, always have planned scenarios to present that you've thought out beforehand. This will help you combat potential surprises, going off on tangents and also consider multiple potential outcomes. Run the scenarios over with trusted colleagues—they will think of things you haven't. Take a little time to practice and prepare just as actors take time to rehearse before they perform.

Rally for the cause: If your team is not behind you, you will not have support or enthusiasm. Get everyone behind you by making sure that your team member's goals and personal interest are in line with your task or goal. The bottom line is, when you get your team to buy into the cause, you'll have a motivated team.

Build a customer base by adding value: "The smartest step you can take to build a customer base, is to focus on value," says Frederick Newell, a well-known marketing strategist. But what does value mean to you and your business? The first thing should be to think about what it means to your customers because customer retention and loyalty should be the primary driver. What do you bring to the table that your customers want and need? That's your value to them, in any type of business, large or small.

Save your customers some time: A study of the Nordstrom department store chain shows that customer surveys indicate they have a reputation for great service. But when they peeled back the layers of the data, it showed the reputation is actually based on merchandise quality and assortment rather than the actual service of the sales associate. So, when you think about this, the data says that Nordstrom is saving their customers time because they don't have to return merchandise; the store is offering them everything they need in one place. It's about "time cost"—giving the greatest possible variety of goods to the customer to save them time so they don't have to shop elsewhere.

Do you have a concern? Let me help: Newell cited how Federal Express built a business out of customer concerns about delivery. The startup did their research and found that shippers had doubts about delivery times of the U.S. post office and of private carriers. They immediately took action and built a business to overcome the concerns of their customers. The slogan "When it absolutely, positively has to be there overnight" was an instant hit and one that the company stood firmly behind.

Do your homework: Always make sure you are conducting studies that focus on what makes your customers happy or unhappy. Also look at what your competitors aren't doing, that customers want.

Separate from the pack: Do you find that many of the companies you do business with are very similar? What separates them? What separates you from your competition? What can you give customers those others don't?

Stay ahead of the curve: Newell's research suggests that you should not be geared to customer behavior as much as toward customer attitudes: Attitude precedes behavior. Attitude is tomorrow's behavior.

Pulse behavior: Online surveying is not new. If you are doing this, are you asking the right questions? Are you asking questions in a friendly manner and with a personal and warm touch? Are you asking questions your specific audience wants to be asked and do you know what that means? If you do your homework, you'll know how to ask the right questions to get the feedback you need to sell the right value.

Stop watching other people win—Your Time is Now!

Today we're living in a world where we are under constantly bombarded with information. There's simply more new data to digest than we can handle. Let's be honest, it can be overwhelming to know how to navigate efficiently with so many new systems and processes today, especially in our hyper speed culture. Add the fact that everything new we create needs to be continuously reengineered and, it can be discouraging, and may want to throw your hands up and say, "Well, why bother?"

That's exactly the kind of thinking you've got to be aware of: it's negative and it drowns your creative and motivational spirit. Instead, when you take action, you are awakening the positive, powerful forces in you. Think of what happens when you take action: you are taking charge of your future. You are forcing yourself to make positive decisions towards what you want to make happen. You are showing resolve and conviction as you exercise your will to do the positive rather than the negative.

It may not look or seem like much, but believe me, it is. Putting these subtle forces into action moves you in the right direction while the opposite achieves nothing. When you "self-start action", this specific process forces you to make choices. For every choice you make, you must take another action. If you make a mistake, you can learn from that; but the process of your decision-making increases to yield better decisions the next time. The more actions you take, the more you improve and boost your chances of becoming more productive.

Tips to Start Preparing your Mind

Take the initiative: Michael Jordan says that one of his secrets of success is, "When I look back, each one of those steps or successes led me to the next one." Now, you don't need Jordan to tell you that, you know this, but we all need to be reminded. When you take action, you are putting yourself in motion; with that comes all the positive effects. Think of it this way: taking action is taking initiative, right? So being proactive versus reactive is a positive thing.

Start with you: Taking initiative simply starts with your mind. Focus on your thoughts, your emotions and willpower. Everyone knows what they want and many know how to get it. But they spend their time procrastinating and daydreaming, saying, "I'll start it next month, next week... or tomorrow." My dad taught me this mantra "tomorrow never comes", which really means "do today instead of doing tomorrow."

Be decisive: When you take the responsibility to focus on what you hope to accomplish and weigh your options, you can be decisive. You can stand by your convictions. You don't need other people's approval because you can set out and achieve your goals with confidence. Taking the initiative can mean being risky, but taking that risk is taking control.

Be assertive: This means taking the time to clearly consider what you are trying to accomplish. It also means summoning your will to take action. I know this can be a little scary but following through and taking action demands strong character traits— discipline, willpower, and leadership.

Focus on doing it *"Right."* You want to make sure you accomplish what you're setting out to do the right way and when you do the above, the results will follow.

Create an Action Plan that Delivers Results

I read a quote when I was young that always stuck with me about preparing goals by writing them down and then taking the time to process it properly: ***"You can't take action until you have a course of action."*** I've always appreciated that advice because preparation is key. Investing the time to chart out your game plan for how you want to achieve something is getting tougher today because we are becoming a faster paced society; but, rarely does a great plan of action come together by "winging it."

Story after story of successful people achieving great things starts with how they charted out a course of action.

How to start your action plan

The first step is to get it down on paper: A great method for charting out your plan is what is called the "Bicycle Wheel and Spoke" approach. In the middle of a piece, draw a circle, then put down your project goal in it. Then draw lines out from the circle (like spokes on a bicycle tire) and write down all the things that you believe can set you back. Now, after you've done that, write down all the solutions to those problems that you listed.

I suggest talking to at least two people you trust so you can make sure you get other people's opinions and find potential setbacks that you hadn't considered. This is a good case of "two or three heads are better than one." The time you put into this is known as developing strategic thinking.

In charting out a plan to achieve your goal, you may find you have to fix a few problems on those spokes first before you get moving on your main goal. That's okay—you are moving in the right direction. Most importantly, you are taking action to get to your goal. Bottom line is that if you want to be "Number One" in anything, you have to map out a strategy and get moving on it today.

In writing down this goal-mapping strategy, you can refer back to it if you forget part of it. Also getting into the habit of writing things down is key. You can store them down in the Notes area of your phone or actually take the old-school approach and buy a journal on which to take notes, some come with a pen holder. Keep these simple tools with you so you can write down ideas on the fly. Start writing down things you hear on your podcasts or see on the internet, or on TV, that correlate to your goals. You'll see this is a positive habit that can help you drive your motivation to achieve your goals on a daily basis.

Surround yourself with the right people: So many coaches give advice that surrounding yourself with the right people will help you get the results you are looking for. Just as a team's success is dependent on the right people, you will have a much higher chance of reaching your goals on your action plan if you surround yourself with people who can encourage and motivate you. If your goal is fitness-related, spend more time with friends or co-workers who actually go to the gym. They will keep you focused on the right actions you want to take. Good people in your personal circle can be encouraging. Choose carefully. People who distract you from your goals or don't believe in you are not the people who will push you to your greater goal achievements.

Break your actions down: After you know where you want to go and you have mapped out the steps and problems you need to tackle before starting, break the overall project into manageable chunks, just as you did with goals in the last chapter. By breaking down projects into each action, you can see the goal clearly and identify what you need to do in the short-term to achieve your overall goals. It's easier to get going and motivated when you break a major activity, or project down like this rather than just looking at the end goal.

Creating this blueprint for success helps you get started right away and allows you to fit manageable pieces into your current schedule.

Failure, viewed wisely, is life's developmental lessons for new decisions

Failure and mindset can fall into many categories in this book. I decided to mention it here in our "making good decisions" chapter. Why? Because I believe that failure, if viewed correctly, is about making the decisions to learn valuable life lessons, each of which is uniquely gifted to you. What you do with those experiences will set the course of where you go in your life. There are leaders who can drive others by reciting an old adage "failure is not an option" but, if taken the wrong way, can put enormous pressure on other people. In fact, too many people have done terrible things to themselves because of the enormous pressures they put on their own shoulders. This is because they have built up something incalculable into their minds about what their failure is going to look like. Far too many of us are not taught to factor in that failure leads to strategic improvement.

Failure is a part of life, and no one goes through life without failing. However, what you do with failure is most important and seeing failure as a life lesson is a mindset that takes time to develop. In fact, just reading it here, won't do enough because you will likely forget the depth of the meaning. I created this book to be something you read periodically as a collection of valuable learning lessons. What's important is that each time you read these lessons; you'll be in a different place in your life. Therefore, you'll be able to reflect on the lesson differently and learn something new.

Think about your favorite game when you were a kid. When you lost the first time did you quit and never play again? Of course not! How many times did you play that game over and over and over - more times than you'll admit, right?! Rather than quitting and walking away, you got better and better and better at the game. In fact, some of you might have become champion caliber players! Life in some ways is like gaming. For every failure you have, you can switch your mindset to that of a learning mindset. You can focus on what went wrong that caused you to fail and by searching for the solution, you can turn failures into valuable personal tools for your success – this is what you want to develop.

In the 21st Century, Failure is the new Resilience for Success

Consider the story of Billionaire entrepreneur, TV personality ("Shark Tank") and owner of the Dallas Mavericks (NBA) Mark Cuban who wrote in his 2013 book, "it doesn't matter how many times you almost get it right. No one is going to know or care about your failures, and neither should you." When you finally get it right, "then everyone can tell you how lucky you are."

Now some of you are thinking "oh great, a story about the guy from Shark Tank; why do I want to read about another billionaire? The answer is, because Mark Cuban might be a billionaire now but he had a whole bunch of failures and probably made more mistakes than you ever will!

In Mark's childhood he had many jobs, just like some of us, and also, like some of us, he probably failed a lot along the way. In fact, many of the jobs he had were the same jobs that most of us had. He was a bad carpenter and as a short order cook and server he was lousy! Even in college his first job was in a computer store but he quit because, get this, he didn't see how computers would be important in the world! Mark tried selling powdered milk but the only people who he sold it to was his parents! I remember hearing that at some point, Mark couldn't earn enough money from any of his many jobs to keep the lights on in his apartment. But Mark's story, like so many others that we see, hear and read about is ultimately about making decisions.

Every single time Mark failed he made a decision to keep trying and to keep going forward. You may only know Mark Cuban as somebody famous on TV or someone who owns a professional sports franchise. Yet, he has even failed in making good decisions on both TV and sports. I bet you didn't know his first TV series was called "The Benefactor" and it was canceled after the first year. Again, remember that Mark says in his own words "No one is going to know or care about your failures, and neither should you."

So, failure was a part of his journey at every level, and it will be part of your life journey as well. The decision you make after any failure is a reflective gift. Now, you get to try something again in a new way, or in several new ways until it works for you. Or, you can take what you learned from failures and try something totally new altogether. The choice is yours; the decision is yours. Keep in mind that success is largely predicated on trial and error, and that means trying and failing before you succeed.

Chapter 7

Don't Limit Yourself, Become a Student of Learning for Life

How we Limit Ourselves

Today we are inundated with so much data that it's almost beyond our ability to keep up. If you try, as so many of us do, you can lose the ability to actually take some of the most important pieces of data and create something useful. Gerard Achstatter a newspaper journalist, wrote a piece stating that studies from some of the biggest companies in finance, manufacturing and technology, show how employees consistently do certain things that undermine corporate performance. He goes on to say that "this underperformance was not due to lack of knowledge but rather by lack of action."

Research by Jeffrey Pfeffer and Robert Sutton on a number of well-known companies finds that: "knowledge fails to be turned into action for several reasons." The following list explains those reasons:

Talking as a substitute for acting: How many meetings have you been in where issues are identified and many ideas tossed out as potential solutions, yet the room can't agree which way to move forward? So, nothing gets done. If we were being honest, the closing remark at the end of the meeting would sound like this: "Thank you all for coming—we've heard lots of good ideas that could solve our problems, but since no one can agree, we'll meet back here when another major blunder happens and re-discuss the same topics again in three months—thanks for everyone's time!"

Why not set up two or three project groups and see which one offers the best ideas and time to implement them after three weeks? Implement two or all three at the same time; see which one starts to show best results. See, the problem is just talking and not taking any action. A strong leader can turn talk into action.

Believing that decisions based solely on past successes can substitute for innovative thinking: This is a trap. This is getting too comfortable in your own doing and thinking. You must think outside the box and change things. Fear of change is one of the biggest human issues that stifles progress.

Letting fear of reprisals prevent sound decision-making based on knowledge: Fear of reprisals is by far one of the biggest reasons why people make a move to another company. People feel they are not being heard. If they present new ideas around their boss, who does not agree with them, they are scared that they will be fired. Not only have I heard this reason from thousands of people who want to move on, I've personally lived in those shoes myself! Have you? We have all kinds of fears when it comes to voicing our ideas:

- Fear of your ideas being knocked down for a bogus reason.
- Fear of someone else in a different, or higher, position taking your ideas and running with them, then getting the credit and the promotion.
- Fear of not being able to talk to your boss's boss's boss even though you hear that he or she is looking for new ideas on how to combat an important issue in your business.

A strong leader has an open-door policy and lets everyone know that credit is given to the person who comes up with the best ideas. The strong leader will listen and bring those ideas to his or her boss, along with the person who originated the idea. Such a leader will make him or herself available to hear other ideas from everyone in the organization—and create a forum for that to happen. If you work for someone with an open- door policy, don't limit yourself with one idea, prepare several, so he or she knows you are someone ready to take action. If you work for someone who thinks he or she knows everything, don't give up - keep learning, and have good ideas at the ready. This way when your time comes to step up, (and it will) you'll be prepared.

Allowing internal rivalry to stifle the sharing of knowledge:
Internal rivalry happens when the issues above occur, and staffers fear that their ideas will be stolen and presented by someone else who will take all the credit. If a lot of rivalry is happening, and no one wants to share ideas, it's a bad thing for the leaders and the organization. Open communications forum can change this, by encouraging and rewarding people's ideas rather than stifling them.

Two huge problems that hold people down:
First, people are afraid that if they make a mistake they will be reprimanded and/or mocked—or even worse. Good leaders will go out of their way to reinforce the outlook that making mistakes in good faith is a positive part of the process. They communicate their support over and over again and they understand that people learn a lot from mistakes.

Second, people throw money at technology to solve problems, or that we hope will solve our problems. Unless you train people to use technology, the people will fail and/or the technology won't work as it should, or it won't be used optimally. Don't let technology run your business, people run a business using the tools of technology.

Pfeffer and Sutton also say there are several ways to help convert knowledge into action:

Use a set of basic business and operating principles:
Strong leaders hold themselves accountable to a high standard. You should too! Don't let outside forces compromise your integrity. Be accountable. If

you set out to follow your principles, but in three months, you're changing your tune, you will lose credibility. Stick to your guns.

Recognize that action counts more than elegant plans and concepts:
Millions of dollars are spent creating fancy PowerPoints, charts and reports. Weeks, months, and business quarters are taken to prepare these reports. Then many times, nothing gets done. As we all know, in business, things typically start from the top. Leaders should recognize that writing a report or making a PowerPoint is just the first step of the process. Creating a plan is good work, but then the hard work should begin and actually work the plan. This is where you can step up and show that you have more to offer beyond just a report or PowerPoint.

Allow for mistakes: At some point, as you gain experience in the business world, you will find yourself in situations in which you will be asked to lead a team or a project. And in nearly every business situation you will find that people make mistakes. The truth is mistakes are inevitable, people are not perfect. Strong leaders make it known time and again, that it is okay for their people to make mistakes. But remember, you can't say that and then pass the buck when something goes down on your watch. You must be accountable. Get in the trenches, and get involved. Make sure your people are given the support they need to solve the problems, too. The key is to accept that we are all fallible and that we will make mistakes. Learning from those mistakes should be seen as growth; those who make honest mistakes should be rewarded for taking chances. Encourage your people to succeed and open the lines of communication. You can't preach letting go of fear if you have it yourself.

Encourage workers to fight the competition not each other: This is one of the biggest issues I've seen: companies allow their own people to fight each other, which leads to holding back information or through voluntary sabotage. Next thing you know, your competition is way ahead and your people leave for better opportunities where they can implement their ideas. Stay focused on the competition, and not each other because the competition out there are the real threat to your company.

To Get to the Top, Get Your Reading On

Some people think that getting a new job is a good time to sit back and relax. After all, you've worked hard to get the new job and you've got a nice increase in pay. Sitting back would be the absolute wrong thing to do. In today's rapidly changing, hyper speed economy, you've got to continue focusing on your own personal growth. Getting a new job is of course great, but you should treat it like week one of a new class in school. It's go-time or you'll get left behind.

Personal growth is critical to your success; and it should be a top priority to you. Even when you are on top of your game, if you let up, you'll soon find you have to play catch up. Things are changing that fast. To be successful means learning about areas of your company outside your business unit. Intellectual curiosity is important when it comes to successfully understanding your organization as a whole.

Today, jobs have become more specialized, which means changing and adjusting to new updates faster and faster each year. Companies are trying out new technologies now more than ever. However, the one thing that can't be bought anywhere else on the street is your brain. Peter Drucker, the management guru wrote, "Knowledge is the primary resource and society's true wealth."

Formal education is just the beginning: When you graduate with your bachelor's degree, that's just the beginning. Kenneth Mahon, a Chief Financial Officer in New York City, said it best many years ago, "School teaches you how to think," and I agree. School is only the beginning of life-long learning. Of course, classes don't teach you very much about the real world, but that's because the real world doesn't run like a well-written book. The real world doesn't flow from chapter to chapter. The real world is chaos. That said, getting a formal education does give you a solid foundation to build upon; it teaches you how to continue learning in the real world.

Make time to read on your own: You simply can't stop learning if you want to get ahead. When I started working as a junior associate, the technical terms both my clients and my candidates were using in conversation was like a different language — and I was new to "tech-speak". That was not okay with me; since my job was to recruit and work with people in technology, then I had to know what they were saying. But how could I without being a techie? So, I started reading industry magazines, specifically focusing on the technologies used by the people I was trying to place in positions. At that time, it was all the variations of UNIX and databases. After some time, I became well versed in tech-talk, and gained respect from CIO's and CTO's who were my clients. They were amazed what I knew, and what I could conceptualize, and what they were talking about; to them it was refreshing that I took the time to read about the systems and new releases. Because of this, I won a lot of business, and my company promoted me every year. When I moved into an area manager role , I did many things to give my employees that added edge as well, I asked all my employees to subscribe and read technology industry magazines too. As a result of their extra reading, our team made rock-star production numbers quarter after quarter, year after year.

Research is fundamental: Learning more about your field of expertise, your organization and industry's niche should excite you. Reading about what's happening in your world should open opportunities for continued learning. Taking online courses at night, a short one- to two-month weekend program or even reading a book released by a scholar in your field are all ways for you to be learning more and propelling your career forward.

Sharing enthusiasm is in demand: If you find a great class or an exciting event that connects to your job, bring it to your manager. Show initiative and passion for adding more value. This strategy can not only help you gain more contacts and relationships in your field, but if you show how you plan to use the knowledge you gain at work; you can convince your company to pay for it.

The Facts Are In: Voracious Readers Climb to the Top

I've read countless stories about successful people, many of whom have a habit of constantly reading. I learned this lesson as a kid during my rebellious years in middle and high school by listening to my dad. Though in many areas of India in the 1940s, families did not keep records of anything, as my mom tells it, he had skipped several grades. He was number one is his class every year. He grew up in the Ganges where they literally had no electricity, which meant he went to the equivalent of the town square to study. He was first class and rank from the now famous IIT Kanpur – a top engineering school in India's largest state called Uttar Pradesh, (UP). When I asked him how he came to America, he said he was the number one student coming out of college so he got out; but the number two guy stayed behind. He earned a scholarship to Massachusetts Institute of Technology (MIT), where he completed his PhD and then won the Alfred Noble Prize, John Chipman Award, and many other honors. Of course, that just annoyed me when I was younger.

But not everyone finishes or even goes to college. Getting ahead in the world doesn't require it. Bill Gates never finished at Harvard University; but the world-renowned founder of Microsoft has always been an avid reader. He reads and gets inspired by other great leaders like Warren Buffett. He has been known to read Buffett's annual letters to his shareholders. I've read that Gates even multitasks by reading while on his exercise bike! So, you can take multiple paths to becoming a voracious reader and knowledge expert – choose what works for you.

How to Understand Your True Self Worth

As you grow, you learn a lot in school, in work and in life, but have you ever wondered what your knowledge is worth?

If you haven't thought about it, you should. Knowing what your brain is worth can help steer you in life towards your educational and career goals. Working on these goals will ultimately define your self-improvement plans and your self-worth.

Think of your brain as a company. A company creates something: products or services. Your brain creates ideas that build those products and services. Therefore, your intellectual capital represents your assets, just as products and services are assets for a company. Talented company managers around the world know their best assets and focus on them, to make themselves more valuable. Do the same for yourself: knowing that your brain is valuable, you should do whatever you can to increase its worth. Smart people focus on the skills they need to increase their worth. Gordon Petrash, a former intellectual capital manager, said it best, "More important than what you know and do is what you will know and will do." He and I agree, especially when he said, "People who value themselves based only on what they know put themselves in danger of being made obsolete." Therefore, I say that what you know plus what you are focused on learning defines your self-worth.

Calculate how much your company benefits from your projects: Keep in mind that just as a company can show revenue or profitability for products, they can also highlight where they have saved money. Were you on a project that created a new product or part of a team that created cost cutting? Maybe you were the head of a project that saved millions of dollars or you were a key member who created a new version of an existing product. See what the company earned or lost, and come up with a value for yourself. Just remember to keep things in perspective. For example, did you do the project yourself and did you fund it? Make sure you keep those factors in mind and give your other colleagues their share of the value as well, and consider the company for their funding and risk taking.

Measure the benefits from your contribution. Ask yourself some questions as part of this exercise:

- How long did the product or service take to bring to market, from concept inception to completion?
- How many people participated on the project?
- What was the level of your responsibilities?

If you're still in school, look at projects that you have done with other people and determine what your value was to the project.

Look at the attributes that separate you from others. List your business and educational achievements.

- Based on your achievements, what can you provide to the next role you are applying for?
- What is required that you do not yet have? If given the opportunity, what proficiencies would you take on personally?

Whatever you lack in education and skills now, is available for you to learn. Education will make your thinking more valuable to employers and to yourself. Education also unlocks the doors to many opportunities. Look at education as a continuing never-ending habit and you'll have continuing, never-ending opportunities.

The Mentor-Mentee Relationship

Today it seems pretty hard to get ahead. Job satisfaction, according to many polls, is not high. With the amount of attention paid to better work environments, we should be happier at work. But we're not. So, many of us think a better-paying job will solve our problems, that a better job title and salary will make us happier. But these are only short-term fixes for happiness. People really should be looking for a better manager from whom they can learn.

Getting a better manager should be easy, right? Yet it's a lot harder than it sounds. Many top managers don't, won't, or can't help the people who work for them. Bradford D. Smart, an adviser to Fortune 500 companies says, "Only one in four bosses is an excellent coach." While companies today are trying to implement better mentoring programs, most are unsuccessful. At the end of the day, like everything else in the life, it's up to you to find a good coach and mentor. Having a good coaching mentor is one of the best things you can do for yourself. "It's more important than salary or responsibility," says Smart. Strong coaching managers can help push top performers to higher levels and pull underachieving workers up with counsel and guidance.

But it's up to you to find someone to help you. Being proactive in searching for a mentor keeps you focused in what you're trying to achieve. It can even help you understand the dynamics you are looking for and steer you toward a new job. With today's social media, it's easier than ever before. And when you do find someone who shows an interest in you, you should be proactive and seize the opportunity.

Smart points out that the mentoring relationship has benefits for the mentor as well as for his or her pupil. Managers can coach by offering training to all employees. They can mentor top employees as well as struggling ones who have potential to better align with the company. The mentee learns new skills and takes on new assignments, which frees managers to tackle projects that will take their own game to a new level.

Numerous studies examine why mentoring has been unpopular thus far; many experts think the relationship creates fear in managers who worry about becoming vulnerable to younger or less expensive competitors. But mentees can reduce these fears by making their managers look great. Those who are good at coaching and have leadership qualities are in greater demand today than ever.

Counseling: Through counseling, struggling employees can gain an opportunity to learn what their bosses want; the lessons can be tough but they are lessons for growth. It's important that the situation is portrayed correctly because people can be defensive about being "counseled." It's hard for people to realize they have shortcomings. When properly presented as an opportunity for learning, struggles can lead to successful and positive relationships. Learn what the boss needs, what would benefit the business and how you can grow. Use counseling to your benefit by setting concrete objectives and highlighting achievements that will come when those objectives are met.

Coaching: This practice is a bit different than counseling; it involves managers giving their employees direct help in learning how to navigate to finish a job or process. Many forms of coaching exist, with varying degrees, including short-term or on-going approaches. The best coaches are those who teach the student how to find answers for themselves. Don't be afraid to seek out coaching if you believe it can help you learn.

Corporate change: Often a company's new direction creates underperformance. For a variety of reasons, many people can't assimilate change. Again, fear can be an obstacle, as employees start worrying what change can mean for them, personally. But everyone must learn to adapt to change in order to survive. Those who adapt can thrive. It's also a company's job to be transparent and highlight why change is needed, and not just how it will help the company but how it will help people individually. Look for books, articles or blogs about changes and transitions at work and select a few to read. Once you better understand change, you will be less fearful of it.

Companies need to pulse their employees' feelings more: Companies can help employees by adding more frequent performance reviews. If you know you are getting semiannual reviews instead of annual reviews, working toward your goal becomes more of a top priority. Ask about receiving a semi-annual review.

Start early on: Right after you start a new job, you should be busy trying to learn from other folks in your company. No person knows everything, not even the CEO. Starting early on helps you form relationships, gets you on the right track to success, and keeps you engaged. You can never start too early when it comes to learning.

Chapter 8

Self-Discipline, Faith, and your Personal Support System

Achieving Self-Discipline in Today's Hyper-Driven World

Are you feeling as though you are missing something that would help you accomplish your goals? You're not alone—in today's fast paced world it's easy to get distracted. We are getting pulled in ten different ways with email, texts, phone calls, alerts, pop-up ads… you name it. And here's the thing: the world is only going to keep moving faster! You can start to manage the insanity by becoming more disciplined and focused on your tasks. The more disciplined you are, the more you'll achieve and the more you achieve the more opportunities you'll create for yourself.

Many motivational speakers have talked about discipline and organization, such as John Maxwell. Along with his books, he was head of the leadership institute, Injoy Stewardship. Maxwell wrote, "When you are disciplined and organized, you move smoothly from one project to the next with no wasted motion. Your priorities are clear." Of course, that statement was made before smart phones and our current hyper speed culture arrived but the principles are still sound; they just need to be tweaked for today.

Many motivational speakers and time management strategists put together great plans. The following paragraphs outline some of the best techniques for developing self-discipline. Use some or all, but the key is to use what you need and put it into immediate action:

List priorities: Numerous coaches have spoken about how trying to do a few things at full steam leads to burnout, wearing down faster while being less effective. Therefore, it's key to be organized right from the start: make a list of priorities, organize each one of your projects in a separate folder, and do one project at a time. In setting up your projects and preparing to do them in order, you will start to see your short-term goals and your long-term strategies come into focus. Top priorities fall into a couple of categories; the first are priorities that which needs to be done quickly because of an external time constraint, like studying for an exam or finishing a report for school or work – you only have x amount of time. The other priorities – especially when it comes to long-term goals, are those steps that must be in place for you to continue moving forward. For example, the foundation of a house must be a priority because you can't build the rest of the house without having it in place.

The best was to start is simply by listing five or six areas in which you lack willpower or self-discipline. Once you get them down on paper, or on your computer, rewrite them again but this time prioritize them in order of importance starting with those that you need to focus on and tackle first. These are the items that must be completed in the shortest amount of time. Then focus on each item separately, one at a time. This is not always possible if you have a couple of items that need to be completed at the same time. But, try as hard as you can not to put too much on your plate at once – otherwise you are more likely get overwhelmed and do a mediocre job.

Educate: Find resources that can help you: audio books, e-learning, podcasts, seminars, conferences, blogs and YouTube videos are just a few choices—whatever works best for you to conquer each area.

Get help: Ask a person whose traits and willpower you admire to give you advice and guidance. Don't know anyone? Join a club or group that meets face-to-face or online. Get to know the people and seek out someone with whom you can establish a rapport. Once you feel comfortable, ask if that person can help you with your goals, mission, or whatever it is that you are focused on achieving. Then, ask that person if they would hold you accountable to what you are trying to achieve.

Take time-outs to focus on your planning and your progress: Develop a plan and set-up a routine so you prepare your upcoming day each morning. At your midday point, take five minutes to review what you've accomplished thus far. Then at the end of the day, make sure to re-evaluate and consider how you did. Look at your list of priorities and check off any that you have accomplished, or at least make a note of the steps you've taken in that direction. This technique requires discipline. The time you make for your daily time and task management can help you tremendously.

Set up a goal and a deadline: Thirty days is a good timeframe for smaller goals. If you need more time after the deadline, set yourself up for another thirty days—but make every effort to meet each goal. These can also be smaller pieces of a larger goal.

Celebrate and recalibrate: How did you do? Any small achievement toward your goal should be discussed with your new friend or mentor. Then do something for yourself; give yourself a reward knowing it is because of your achievement. Let your friend, mentor or anyone helping you know that you appreciate their efforts. Now it's time to move onto the next area you've written down.

*** After you start executing the action items above and you see incremental results that propel you forward, you'll be surprised how you ever went through life without being organized and productive. Doing these things will keep you on the right track ***

Expect things to go wrong: Life is crazy and things rarely go 100 percent as planned – if you know that from the start and get in the habit of expecting something to go wrong, you'll be better able to handle your stress level when problems pop up. As we mentioned in the last chapter, mistakes are inevitable. But when things do go wrong – and they will – you won't be taken by surprise if you're prepared, and you'll be able to take a deep breath, and work on doing whatever is necessary to get back on track.

Know thyself: When are your peak productivity hours? Recognize when you are at your best and make sure to optimize that time. Put your secondary tasks, or lower priority items on your list, into hours when you are winding down.

Believing in Yourself Counts Most

I only heard of Steve Allen while writing this motivational book, but after learning about him, and astonished by his accomplishments, I knew I wanted to add him to this manuscript. At age twenty-five, Allen was traveling across the country doing his comedy radio show. By age twenty-six he was out of work and took the only job he could find, which was spinning records at an L.A. radio station. While spinning at the radio station worked hard creating the concept and format for a new TV show and within two years, he had created his program: a one-hour comedy talk show.

Allen's work and perseverance led to a variety talk-show on CBS television network from 1950 to 1952 and soon after a late-night talk show on NBC's flagship TV station in New York. NBC, at the time, was looking to pair its popular talk show, "The Today Show," with an evening talk show and Allen's talk show become so popular they renamed his show, "The Tonight Show" and let him create the format. This led to one of the longest running, popular shows in the history of television and Allen's personal five-decade long career in the TV business.

Allen's secret? "I don't waste time," he said when interviewed back in the day at age seventy-seven. "I work seven days a week. The work I do is so pleasurable there would be no point (in stopping) simply because something called 'a weekend' has been reached."

A multi-talent, Allen was a comedian, author, lyricist, composer, and playwright. He built his career on four tried-and-true but often forgotten principles:

When you're dealt lemons, make lemonade: Allen was the star of a dozen TV series. That's a lot of great TV but also that means he received a bunch of cancellation notices. He was never fazed by a cancellation; for example, when his prime-time NBC variety show series was cancelled in June 1960 after four years of production, he was back on TV at another network the next year. When commercial television hit harder times in the late 1970s, he created a hit series called "Meeting of Minds" on Public Broadcasting Systems that ran for four years.

Get out of your own way: "At the moment of creativity, don't second guess yourself," Allen notes. "All the editing, revising, and improvements can come later—when you've got a great idea, get on it, get it down, and stay with it." When I finally started writing, I'd had the idea for my book for more than ten years. That's a lot of time I could have been writing. Now, I just start writing and work on revising them later. If you are too cautious, as I was, and you're not sure about yourself, look at Steve Allen's strategy and the output: he got out of his own to way and produced fifty-three books, six musicals, four plays, and fifty-two record albums. Now, that is a great portfolio of assets.

Free yourself from restrictions: Steve Allen wrote more than 7,200 songs. Yet - get this: he can't read music! In 1985, the Guinness Book of World Records listed him as "the most prolific composer of modern times." More than eighty artists have performed his hits, including Aretha Franklin, Tony Bennett, Ella Fitzgerald, and Lionel Hampton. The morale is: just because you can't do everything well, doesn't mean you can do many things well.

Keep it fresh by changing it up: As an author, Allen definitely received his share of rejections but as he notes, "Just about everything I write does seem to eventually get published." He says that one of his tricks is variety. This rings a bell for me personally, I write about a few main topics but I try writing outside of my scope as well. At work, I branch out and get involved in other business areas that can impact my business unit.

Be Truthful to Yourself and End Procrastination!

You've probably got a favorite excuse—or several—that you can think of for not following through. We all do! How many projects or agenda items did you postpone or stop working on over the years? Take a moment and write down everything you are still working on from the last few years. Now, write down your excuses for not finishing them. The best part is you're only telling yourself about these excuses, so there's no shame. Or is there? Are there one or two excuses you wrote down for more than one of your unfinished projects? Now, write a short list of successful people who did great things against all odds that you admire. Do you think they would use the excuses you wrote down?

Want to follow through more effectively? "End the excuse marathon," advises behavioral researcher William Knaus. He believes you can start shattering the myths below by ending procrastination in many ways:

I work better under pressure: It seems easier to work under pressure, because by waiting until the last possible minute, you're forced to keep working until the project is done," said Knaus. He's right you know—about feeling forced to work under pressure. When I did my undergrad schooling, I always found friends in the class and we ended up pulling "all-nighters," staying up studying and drinking soda and coffee then going to take the exam in the morning. But when I did my MBA, I studied from day one. I never pulled "all-nighters" and it was much easier to get A's. I learned from my mistakes and made a point of taking academic achievement a high priority.

The fact is, it's not easier to work under pressure. You're straining your mind and body by rushing to get your work done which could lead to more errors and you won't have the time to do double checks on your work either.

If I put this off, the world isn't going to end, so it can wait: Sure, the world won't end, we all know that. But the longer you put off work and tasks, the more likely someone will, for example, beat you to the punch and finish what you don't or come up with the same idea as you. Ask yourself how many times you were too afraid or too lazy to open your mouth in a meeting when there was a call for fresh ideas? How often did you remain quiet while someone else said what you were thinking? Sucks, doesn't it?

I'll do a better job when I'm in a better mood: Waiting for inspiration, or a change of mood isn't the best way to get moving. It's the other way around. "Inspiration usually follows action," says Knaus. When you do a project, it leads to idea generation—even just the beginning of action can start a whirlwind of ideas. When you start to gain momentum and follow through on tasks and action items, it will become habitual.

I'll start the project tomorrow—I can't miss the social engagement: I remember saying that to myself all the time in college – "I can't miss the event tonight"—instead of studying. I'm sure I would take back some of those choices if I could.

I can put this project off to the last minute; that way I won't have to spend much time on it and I can do something else now: A few things are happening here: doing work beforehand and getting ahead lets you find problems and resolve them. By pushing it off, it stays in the back of your mind, and is a subconscious stressor that quite frankly, you don't need. And, if something unexpected pops up, you could end up out-of-time.

This project seems overwhelming: To make a project less overwhelming, try breaking a project down into manageable parts as you've been learning in this book already; it's a great way to work. It allows you to focus on one piece at a time, which makes your work load easier and lets you see things more clearly too - because you have more time to contemplate.

I would have done the project sooner but "this and that" event happened and I couldn't control it: Events are part of life and how you respond to them is the key. While some things are truly out of your control, many are not. When you learn how to manage your responses to various situations and events, you'll find yourself being more productive. Then this excuse simply vanishes.

How to Keep on Keepin' On: I agree with famous thinkers like Knaus that the foundation of the whole process starts when a person realizes and admits that procrastination exists within them. When you can look yourself in the mirror and say, "It's really me, but I am ready to fix this," then you are ready to start the journey of high productivity and pull a 180 on yourself. Here are a few ways to help:

Take inventory: Take inventory on the areas in which you lack confidence or are less effective. Be honest – it's okay to admit shortcomings, that's how you determine where you need to improve and what you need to learn.

Find your bottom floor: When you can face up to your faults, then you'll be better at working through stress, fear, frustrations, and setbacks. You need to stop making excuses and retracting into the comfortable space of not doing anything! The reality is that it's okay to have faults. Accept faults and weaknesses as part of adult development. The acceptance alone is something very positive many people can't do – they never find a starting point from which to start personal development. That said, finding it can be very motivating when you consider what you will achieve when you overcome your weaknesses. We all have a desire to become better, why not find your bottom floor and work upwards? How inspiring to build your 2.0 self!

Emphasize your strengths: No one is perfect and no one will be. So, when you are working to better yourself, remember the positive things you are capable of doing. Highlight your positives in an interview. Make sure you tell your boss that even when you are not 100 percent qualified for that bump up, you still bring a lot to the table. Don't stop reminding yourself of your worth and let others know it too.

Know if there's pain, there will be gain: Tackling some projects are a pain in the butt. However, you know the outcome of the time invested *has to* get you ahead. Short-term discomfort can take you to the next level, which is a long-term reward. A great example is starting or finishing an educational degree or program. Yes, it's a lot of work during that time, but it will mostly likely pay off for many years to come.

I'll give *myself* five minutes—that's it! Commit to giving yourself five minutes to start doing the project or action item you've been pushing off. After five minutes, decide if you want to keep going. Knaus said, "Once you get into something, there's a human tendency to bring closure to it." He goes on to elaborate: "You're working psychology to your advantage and have a stronger chance of completing the project."

Build Your Own Support System

The most famous people, whether they are Olympians, movie stars, billionaire business owners, or notable athletes, have success stories that include persistence, which propelled them to the top.

In today's world of information-overload, as well as cultural clashes and globalization, you need all the help you can get to succeed and stay on the right track. Having a strong support system around you is vital.

Here are some examples of what you can do to stay happy, focused and above all, minimize stress:

Work colleagues: Having workmates can keep you motivated. We spend a lot of time working today, more than ever before. You've got to have colleagues you trust, who you can bounce ideas off of and who keep you focused. The company AIM Management Group was started by Ted Bauer and a few of his colleagues. In the beginning it was challenging for them to keep going but they had a slogan, "Starvation is not an option." The guys stayed focused—according to Bauer: "It was persistence that kept us going." The company grew to be worth $101 billion before being sold to Invesco.

Family and friends. I love the story of Zig Ziglar. I got a chance to meet him many years ago. A well-known U.S. motivational speaker, Ziglar grew up struggling. He sold aluminum cookware door to door. I can stop right here and tell you that if you think your job is tough, think of what Ziglar did for a living. Anyhow, he had encouragement from his wife; he knew she always believed in him. Ziglar said, "I can't tell you what it meant to have a cheerleader cheering for me every day and praying for me every night." Family and friends who pick you up and keep you going is, as MasterCard says, "Priceless."

Faith and belief: Nothing can help you more than a belief in something guiding and watching over you. Do you have a strong belief in a higher power? Do you spend time praying, or talking to whatever you believe in that gives you strength? Having a belief that something is greater than you and you are not the "end-all-be-all" is important and realistic to many people. There is nothing wrong with knowing you do not have all the answers. Unexplainable things have been put in your path because of more than luck; they've saved you from bad scenarios; they may be the reason you exist.

The next time your day is not going as planned, taking a moment for yourself and asking your higher power, whatever that may be, to be with you through your day is more than okay—it could be the best thing you can do. If you don't believe in a higher power, that's okay, choose a friend or family member to talk to, for no other reason but to hear their voice —even for a few minutes. At least you did it. Seriously, you should never be so busy that you can't do this for yourself.

Chapter 9

Resilience, Persistence, Attention to Detail

Resilience in Times of Disruption

In today's day and age, everyone knows what it feels like to be knocked down. But successful people get back up. After going through the past recessions, wherever you were in your life, you've felt some kind of stress or change. Maybe it was a job loss, a reduction in pay, losing co-workers—you name it and you felt some level of disruption. If you were not working at the time, as a teen, maybe you had parents, uncles, aunts or older siblings that experienced such a disruption in their work and life. A large population of teens can remember the issues that their parents went through during the hardship of the most recent Great Recession of 2008. Psychiatrist and author Frederic Flach wrote about how resilience becomes self-perpetuating. "I've seen those who've survived the most heinous prisoner-of-war camps, who have survived a number of serious, adverse events in their lives. Each time they have come back stronger than before."

If you didn't set a New Year's resolution this year but are looking for something to improve on, then try resilience. Here are some tips to help:

Give yourself a stronger sense of self-esteem: When you don't get your way at work, or your project gets knocked down by your boss, don't let it be the end-all-be-all. Don't put your work on the shelf. Strategize around ways to tie your project to other things your company is doing. Realize that the setback is only temporary and that your ideas might circle back in three, six, twelve months. Keep doing your research and keep telling yourself that the time will come when your ideas are relevant. Be patient. When that time comes, you'll be ready with the current trends and can assume a leadership role. This is true for all situations, not only at work. The report you were going to write for a class, but wasn't appropriate, may be a great idea for the next course you take a year from now – keep your ideas in your files.

Be open-minded. Having an open mind means being open to "listening" to another idea that is opposite of yours. That does not mean you have to agree! When you listen, don't have your guard up, and don't simply plan how you will react when the person is done speaking. Instead, while *actually listening,* let your mind create a potentially new idea that neither you nor the person speaking has come up with. That is how new ideas and mutual "meet in the middle" brainstorming works. I don't have to tell you that we can all use a little more of this today.

Know when to separate thought and action: We all work with people who do not think like us. To develop a strong sense of self-reliance, it's important to be able to listen and tolerate advice and opinions on how to do things. But it's just as important to know when to ignore opinions and go with your gut to reach your own conclusions. Bottom line, do your homework and go with your beliefs if you know it's the right thing to do.

Develop a stronger level of tolerance: Disruption is happening everywhere. Change is happening daily, hourly. You can experience drama, turmoil, and setbacks regularly, which can cause real frustration and strong emotions every day. Learn not to ignore them; reliance depends on your ability to recognize pain and constructively deal with it.

Practice self-discipline: About self-discipline, Flach said, "It's the determination to stay focused, to do what has to be done, regardless of difficulty or time constraints."

How can we learn to be more resilient? Start doing a little more of each of the below suggestions and prepare to be amazed at yourself:

Study more: As we discussed in the last chapter, continuing to educate yourself is so important. Don't just read articles and posts on the internet—that does not count. Take the time to enroll in a program. Start small, with a night course or an online course. That's all it takes to get you on your way. Start today with a small but serious effort and you'll soon find yourself at the end of the journey—ready to take on the next one.

Anticipate the future: Keeping up with today's trends is vital to spotting shifts in your industry or company. Read internet trade articles and join groups. Get involved.

Turn negatives into positives: Want to go back to school but not sure what to study? An education program gets you over hurdles with skills and trades that address your weaknesses. Don't just take an easy class, take one that challenges you, so you can improve in areas at which you need improvement.

Cultivate a barrier against pain and suffering: Underemployment has been rampant across the U.S. workforce for the past two decades. Many of us have suffered major setbacks. But it's more than that. Today, more than ever, we are surrounded by prejudice, stubbornness, and ignorance—not to mention the constant spinning of lies which in 2017 were even called *alternative facts*. How do you build your strength as a force of thinking and abilities to stay ahead of the pack? Learn how to meet disappointments and negative circumstances (whether beyond your control or not) by building up your traits of resilience, like self-esteem and self-discipline. It will allow you to get through the tough times.

It is more important than ever to find and cultivate resilience within yourself. You'll be a happier person—and at the end of the day, is there anything else that is more important that your emotional health and well-being?

Obstacles in Life Abound, Go Above and Around for Success

A guy named Stephen Cannell had an amazingly hard time getting through school. Because of his poor reading skills, he had to repeat the first and fourth grades. When he was about to enter fifth grade, administrators asked him to leave. His teachers believed him to be a failure.

When his parents put him in another school, a remedial school, they blamed his poor reading on his vision (even though his eyesight was 20/20). In high school Cannell failed out of the tenth grade and had to repeat that too, but at a different school because again he was asked to leave. He finally graduated at the bottom of his class.

Luckily, during all this time Cannell was struggling with his reading, he focused on the strengths he possessed—athletics. Because of this he won a football scholarship to the University of Oregon in 1961. There he met a teacher who noticed Cannell had some talent and had him focus on creative writing. Cannell explained; "I always wrote to entertain myself. Being perfect on paper never entered my mind."

After graduating from college, again at the bottom of his class, and with little interest in his family's interior design business, Cannell started writing. He worked on his craft, the craft that, with all his struggles in the reading department, had been an albatross around his neck up to that point in his life: "I started out doing it one hour a night, then two. I kept at it and eventually was working up to five hours a night writing TV and movie scripts, short stories, you name it—writing became my passion."

In time, Cannell began selling pilot episodes for television shows to studios. Pretty soon he was regularly writing pilots and pitching ideas for new shows to producers. He ended up creating many shows like "The Rockford Files," and "Baretta." By the time he became famous he had also written multiple novels.

How did this happen to a boy who was consistently told he was a failure, who consistently flunked and repeated grades? How on earth did a boy who was outcast because he couldn't read become a famous writer?

He did it because his parents believed in him. Every time a school told him to leave, his parents put him in another school. What kept this boy's spirits alive when everyone told him he was no good and could not read? "Sports and my dad, were my support outlets, they kept my self-esteem from taking a nose dive," explained Cannell. And what about his vision being blamed for his poor reading, even though it was 20/20? At age thirty-five, Cannell was properly diagnosed with dyslexia.

In life there will always be people who quickly judge you, and most of them have no right to do so. They will not help you succeed. What would you do if you had to go through twenty years of people calling you a failure because you were misdiagnosed? I'm sure many of you are thinking, "Wow, it must have been tough."

The good news is that you can build a support group so you can succeed. Steve Cannell provides a real-life story of persistence and support. You don't need an army of people—just a few of the right people in your corner cheering you on, and a strong belief that you can and will do great things and never give up.

Another Famous favorite example, Ray Kroc, builder of McDonalds Corp., and this man could have given up many times; he was rejected so often he literally became sick. Sometimes he visited multiple investors on the same day. Imagine being rejected on an interview in the morning, having someone say you are no good, and then having to muster enough moxie to wash your face and then hear someone else say the same thing in the afternoon? Now imagine it happening day after day after day. Think of how hard it was back then to get people to listen to you and read about you before the internet. There's a quote by American Essayist and philosopher Henry David Thoreau, that says, "What people say you cannot do; you try and find you can." Consider that we would never have McDonalds, a world-renowned brand, if it wasn't for Kroc's incredible persistence.

Think Fast–Right Now! Or Maybe Not?

People in business today are in overdrive, so we do business and make decisions even faster than before. That's why more than ever you should study every detail that affects your life and your career—since you'll be spending more than half your life doing it.

If you look at what the top leaders do, in poll after poll, that's what they do. Most executives rate their attention to detail in the high or very high category; it's a top factor for success in most polls, too. Yet attention to detail runs counter to today's incessant need to get things done faster. People who take time to make the right decisions instead of quick judgements, however, will be better off.

For example, when you are dealing with people: whether it's employees, customers, or even friends in a social group take time to understand their different points of view, and then consider whether they are making a quick decision or a good decision. It's necessary to take time to make decisions that allow for the broader scope that satisfies many while also being sensible enough to allow for adjustments. Making tough decisions takes time; you can't process all the ethical and social implications, along with the information, with a quick thought.

You might be asking, "what if I don't have the luxury of taking time and have to make quick decisions on the fly?" That's fine; we all have to make quick decisions—it's part of life. But the best leaders separate the "snap" decisions from those that require more time. That separation lets them take extra time to study the details, to contemplate, to make sure they've thought through the many implications that affect us today. A proper decision must be appropriate, social, global, and ethical—but also flexible for minor tweaking that will surely be coming tomorrow.

Numerous studies show the importance of taking the time to analyze details is key. When you fail to study details, you'll make more mistakes. You'll miss critical information, which leads to substandard results. One of the biggest benefits of spending time analyzing details is considering the financial aspects.

Numbers and money, even the littlest amounts, should mean something in any business decision— and both can add up. When you keep making little errors to get things done for the sake of getting them done, they can come back to bite you—maybe even on your annual performance review.

Today it seems everything must be done by "close of business today." I understand it's all about metrics today, but if avoiding unnecessary mistakes is really more important, and it should be.

Seeking advice from a trusted colleague who will purposely keep you from rushing during a decision is a great way to ensure better decision-making in this never-ending process:

Let's Play Devil's Advocate
Have you considered the alternatives?
Have others offered opinions you don't want to hear?
Has someone asked you questions you have not considered?

At the end of the day, the decision is yours and it's what's on your plate. No one should make your decisions for you but securing good advice and bulletproofing your decisions gives you peace of mind. *And having peace of mind—now there's something priceless.*

Life is a Series of Setbacks But It's Really Training for Success

When I get down about being rejected for something, I often think about the story of Jack Ma, founder of Alibaba. He failed and was turned down so many times, it isn't even funny. If you research innovative people for a few weeks, you'll find many examples not unlike Jack Ma's. One of my favorite stories about persistence, resilience and believing in yourself comes from him. Here is a guy, who is in business today and is internationally popular. Yet, if you look at his past, he failed elementary school twice, and in middle school three times (I know that feeling because I was held back once). He then failed his university exams three times and got rejected from Harvard 10 times. He should have been admitted on persistence alone! Today Jack Ma is one of the richest people in the world; a huge Tech Giant. He is the founder of Alibaba. He has been on *Time* magazine's 100 most influential people and was selected as one of China's most powerful people by *Business Week*.

While growing up poor in Hangzhou China, Ma became passionate about learning the English language. Once he became proficient in English, he started giving U.S. tourists staying in high end hotels tours, back in the 1970s. In fact, one of the tourists with whom he became friends, gave him the English name Jack.

As I mentioned earlier, Jack failed miserably throughout his early years. He scored less than one percent in his math proficiency, but with persistence he eventually passed. He also kept failing to get his career started. Consider this; apparently out of 24 people who applied to work at KFC he was the only one that got rejected! He then tried to be a police officer but was turned down. Eventually he became an English teacher making just $12 a month. Yes, $12 a month!

He also struggled while trying to get the e-commerce life, for which we know of him today, off the ground. He first came up with the idea to create an online store because he couldn't find Chinese beer online while doing an online search. So, Ma created a second search engine called China Paige which drew a lot of attention. But when he partnered with the Chinese government, they eventually took control of the business.

Having given up at one point, Ma took a government job with the Foreign Trade and Economic Cooperation Ministry. This led to influential connections such as one with the founders of Yahoo's Jerry Yang. So, in 1999 he left the government job, gathered a group of buddies and they pitched the idea to start an online marketplace for small and medium-sized companies. That led him to get funding, but not before he was rejected in Silicon Valley when he first pitched his online marketplace. Eventually, through great persistence, he got funding from Goldman Sachs and SoftBank.

For Jack Ma and his Alibaba company, there were many grueling years. The business was not profitable at first, and he actually filed for bankruptcy. He lost some of his venture start up colleagues, who walked out on him, instead of pushing on. But with his relentless persistence and by not allowing failures to be a distraction, which became his life's motto, he did some amazing things like growing Alibaba to a point where he was able to drive eBay out of China.

Finally, after fifteen years, he was able to get Alibaba to an IPO in 2014. It was the largest IPO at the time.

So, no matter how young or old you are, this is a story of resilience and incredible failures that, through ongoing persistence led to great success. Jack Ma built an iron clad shield of grit and the most powerful thing of all, a story of believing in yourself for the ages.

Find the people who are innovative, who are game changers that you connect with. Make them part of your personal support structure so when you get down, you can refer to their stories. Then, pick yourself up and get back in the game!

Chapter 10

Making Good Decisions

Success and Survival in Nature Translates to Business

If you think business is tough, think about life in the wild. The difference between success and failure can be razor thin—life and death. In business, just as in the wild, success comes down to the details.

In an article about the National Outdoor Leadership School (NOLS), I learned how they teach mountain climbing and kayaking along with wilderness survival skills to the public. Many of the lessons used at NOLS for outdoor activities, can be used in the workplace as well.

When students complained about being cold and wet to Sam Talucci, a part-time instructor at NOLS, he told them "Watch what the instructors are doing." Talucci instructed his students to "analyze closely how expedition leaders conduct their business." By the time a week or so had passed, all the students were mimicking the instructors—they may not have known why they were doing things like putting on their wet suit at that time, but they did it. "Eventually students get a sense of when they need to take action on their own."

This is no different from how I watched my first managers in business. I learned the littlest things by observation, which might seem silly, but they weren't. When I started my first job, I would go with my colleagues to the deli where we'd get these huge delicious sandwiches. I was always lethargic after that, barely able to function: I specifically remember having to watch a bunch of training videos and wishing I was employed in Spain and could take a siesta. I didn't learn to break my habit of eating too much at lunch and being more productive from my co-workers—I learned from my manager's manager. She ate at her desk, and it was always like a half-lunch portion. I've been doing that for a long time now. She also never stayed in the lunch room where there was a spread of baked sweets and co-workers always hung out, sometimes long after the lunch hour. Everyone but the president hung out in there. I learned not to. I went in, filled up my water bottle and left. I was known for not having a sweet tooth and not having a lot to gossip about. I was also known for breaking many monthly quota production records too. Bottom line, you can learn a lot by watching your role models.

At NOLS, Talucci explained that students learn how to make waterproof, windproof tents out of a single piece of nylon fabric. "In order for the tent to work correctly, though, students must crease, fold and hang the fabric exactly right—the margin of error is tiny. Students who practice pitching the tents repeatedly, until they master every single crease, fold and pull are the ones who remain dry when the snow begins to fall."

It's no different in business; just ask any top producing sales manager. When we trained in the agency, we rehearsed the same rebuttals over and over. After we became managers, we held those same trainings. We discussed the rebuttals several times a week. A few years into working at my first agency, the new folks who went through training once told me it was amazing to hear me on the phone because I had a rebuttal for everything.

Another NOLS alumnus, Tom Scott, who was also a cofounder of the beverage company Nantucket Nectars, gave some good advice about dealing with a crisis: "In the middle of a storm, your ability to calmly walk through the issues is really going to determine your ability to succeed." Scott continued by saying, "Adrenalin can help you in a lot of situations— but in [others], it really creates the opposite effect."

I agree that adrenalin is probably great in many outdoor situations but it might not help in many work situations. Today, more than ever, it's important to remain calm and think things through at work. The ability to not react, to take a few hours to calm down and focus on the details allows us to make more even-keeled decisions. Keep in mind, we see things through our own lens. Take a moment to think through how other folks see a situation.

The last NOLS alumnus, Archie Clemins, a retired admiral, gave advice on teamwork and his ability to analyze his team. If he noticed that a teammate lacked the physical strength to pull a sixty-pound sled uphill, he would step in and carry the pack during the uphill portion of the day's trip.

At one of my agencies at which I worked, we worked in a system that was very team-focused. We relied on each other. If someone on my recruiting team was out sick, we would submit that person's candidates for them. If someone was out to lunch and a call came in—we picked up that client or candidate and talked to that person. It was the best system I've ever seen or been a part of. We broke all kinds of monthly quota production records, could barely keep up with the business our clients kept dishing out to us, and were awarded many vacation trips for breaking quotas. Everyone was super happy in the environment. Best of all, we knew we had each other's backs.

Learning How to Have Role Models That Matter, and Eliminate the Ones That Don't

We do love our role models and today there are so many people that we look up to, for so many different reasons. Role models do many things and we love them for their inspiration because they challenge us and in turn, for some of us, they consciously dare us to be better. Another reason we love role models is because we envy what they do and how they do it. Very often, role models are doing things that are very noble, such as fighting for a group of people who are marginalized. These role models are trying to make the world a better place.

Reshma Saujani who founded Girls Who Code serves as a terrific example of a role model. While she may not be a household name to many baby boomers or even Generation Xers, if you're a young girl who codes you probably know about her. Reshma was inspired to start Girls Who Code after observing inequality and a vast disparity of access to computers while working as an attorney at the 14th District of New York City, which encompasses both a very wealthy community as well as some of the city's poorest residents. Reshma was also surprised to learn that there was a wide gender gap in technology.

To make a difference, Reshma set out to form Girls Who Code back in 2012, and she has been reaching thousands and thousands of girls through after school and summer programs ever since. It all started when she decided to put 20 girls in a room to see if she could teach them how to write a computer program and she saw the results, which were tremendous. She also saw girls building things that were all about improving their communities.

Reshma Saujani is a great example of someone who is trying to make the world a better place. That is a key ingredient for being a role model. We need more role models who are getting involved with communities. They are what we need most, as opposed to more role models who we envy because they have a lot of money. There's nothing very noble about simply acquiring assets.

So how can you set yourself up to find role models that matter to you? As you've come to see, I'm often asking you to write things down. So, in a journal, take some time to consider some key things - are you ready?

Consider, what actually matters most to you? Think about it for a while. Consider all the things that make you happy, consider the things that are meaningful to you, and what you want to spend more of your time focusing on. The world has so many things going on that need to be fixed, but you have to realize that you can't tackle everything. Focus on some things that you really care about, things you previously might not have taken the time to think about. This is the first step. It's not necessarily easy and cannot be done quickly in 20 minutes, or perhaps not in a few days. It could take a couple weeks or even months, but the key is to think about it and write it down. You owe it to yourself to take the time to find out what makes you tick.

Now, based upon your skills, your expertise, and how you can use your abilities to make the world a better place, ponder questions like:

What could I do if I had more knowledge about the subject that I care about? What should I set out to learn, and where can I learn it?

The beautiful thing now is that you know you can spend time doing research on search engines and will have everything you need to learn right at your fingertips. You can research which groups are focused on the things that you want to do and you can join those groups and connect yourself with the people that have the resources and the funds in this space you are interested in. This is the beginning of how you move yourself closer and closer to making your dreams a reality. You can also see, first hand, some of the people that are doing things to make the world a better place. And much like girls who loved computers and coding found Reshma Saujani, who became their role model, you may find yours. While you do your research, remember to write things and start journaling more often because as you grow and as time goes on, you will continue to develop what actually matters to you and how you want to make the world a better place.

Learn What It Means to Make Really Good Decisions and Stop Making Bad Ones

Too many folks still worry about this new age of artificial intelligence (AI). How did we get so worried about AI, for example, taking our jobs? Part of our concern is because of human errors and biases. We all think we have great decision-making skills, right? If you do your research, you'll find many studies by psychologists pointing to weaknesses in how most people make decisions.

But, fear not. With an open mind you can learn to make better decisions. According to Max Bazerman, a professor of Management at Northwestern University, studies have shown that people give more weight to recent events than those from a long time ago. "Such thinking causes people to make blind decisions," he said. This is so true. I've been in talent acquisition for twenty years; it's an unfortunate state that society looks only at the most recent experience of a person to judge whether they are qualified for a position. It happens all the time. I've personally been told that many of my excellent accomplishments managing teams in my past, do not count because it was too far back in my career. I've often thought, *why should that matter?*

It's not as if those prior years of team management became "rotten" like a tomato sitting in the sun. If you thought back to some of your greatest past accomplishments and someone told you those didn't count because you, did it five years ago, it probably would not sit well with you, either. Imagine telling Michael Jordan or Joe Namath that their individual championship efforts didn't count because they did it a long time ago? Yet, we do this to each other in business all the time. It's time to stop making bad decisions because of our biases and start making good ones as intelligent human beings. Or we can let AI make intelligent decisions for us.

Bazerman suggests several reasons why people make suboptimal decisions; let's look at a few of them:

- We are often quick to give someone credit for doing something more recently than if they had done the same or similar work in the past.
- We tend to view ourselves in an overly positive light.
- We are unrealistically optimistic about our future.
- We exaggerate our control over random events.

This kind of thinking, and taking too much credit for ourselves, creates false lessons and ideologies. When we think we can do no wrong and that we're infallible, we make bad decisions based on that fallacy. We may recall scenarios in which people made poor decisions and stuck to it, even after evidence showed impending negative outcomes. We are also not too good at admitting when we are or were wrong, are we? Still wondering why AI is getting so much attention?

Let's look at another interesting decision-making issue that causes risk, which is called "satisficing." This is the process whereby we stop at the first logical answer to a problem rather than continuing to do thorough research or working to find the best possible solution. A good example would be a corporate recruiter looking for a candidate: if a recruiter has twenty candidates in her pipeline, she may find three that fit her criteria in the first ten resumes. Because she is under a tight deadline to deliver quickly—and because she is being judged on how fast she can produce results, she doesn't evaluate all the twenty resumes and stops looking after she's found the three, so, she presents those as her top three candidates and ignores the remaining ones. Was there a diamond in the rough, as they say, who was overlooked? Chances are excellent that there was one – statistically speaking, as well. There's a fifty percent chance that there are three good candidates in the second set of ten resumes, which is a high percentage that can't be ignored – but we do. That is why we have to stop trying to move so quickly that we don't do a thorough job. It's this "need for speed" that's running rampant across everything we do today.

So, how do we develop our abilities to make better decisions? Simply said, it's hard, like most things in life. Bazerman formalized a process by suggesting these steps to improve your decision-making ability:

- Define the problem
- Identify the criteria
- Weigh the criteria
- Generate alternatives
- Rate each alternative on each criterion
- Compute the optimal decision

To give a quick example of utilizing a process to make decisions, I point out my desire to write my first book. A couple of my former employees who had gone on to become managers in different companies asked me to write some LinkedIn posts on exactly these kinds of self-motivated actionable lessons. They did so because at their new places of employment, the folks that they were reporting to were not inspiring them, and as a result they were not inspiring to their subordinates. So, I did, but after a short time, a couple more of my former employees mentioned the same problem of being uninspired at work. In identifying the criteria, I took out a journal and wrote down dozens of identifiable problem areas that might be causing leaders to be uninspiring to their teams. It took some time for sure, but after weighing which ones seemed like the most impactful, I distilled my list down to a more manageable group. Then it was important for me to come up with the right chapter titles and that required me to spend considerable time wordsmithing – generating alternatives. Heck, I even wrote 50 titles for this book!

Finally, I put together several groups of trusted colleagues and asked them for their opinions on a host of different themes and thoughts when I was stuck trying to decide an "either or" chapter for moving forward on writing ideas. In other words, I ran my ideas by a group of people that I trusted to make sure my thinking was headed in the right direction. When you ask a group of your trusted colleagues to weight your ideas and take the time to ask exactly the same questions in the same way, you are doing your own qualitative study and when you get a favorable majority support, you are better able to compute an optimal decision. See? You can do this too. But be sure to run ideas past people whom you really trust to be honest before basing decisions on their feedback.

Of course, we can't go through these steps for every decision we make. Who has time for all this, right? True, but isn't the spectrum of having to re-do things correctly better than going all the way through the process to complete failure? Isn't that much a catastrophe? If a decision is important, then time for proper processes to take shape should be considered.

Here are some tactics for when you don't have time to process a big decision, or the decision is not as serious:

- Train yourself in decision making so it becomes more natural to you and part of how you process decisions. For example, try Six Sigma or Agile methodology.
- Talk to your peers, bounce ideas off them and ask them to play devil's advocate. It works.
- Avoid one of the biggest defenses we use, "Sorry, I've been so busy." It's a poor excuse, and you will always be busy. You could say we are all so busy we don't have time to "think." That is a scary state to be in. Stop creating a world around you where you can't come up for air and actually think. The last decade was all about how AI and technology will make humans better and some folks even said "AI will make humans more human." I say no, AI systems are advanced support for us, and its time we embrace getting back to being superior in our reflective, strategic and design thinking capabilities. Or, you can simply plug yourself into the matrix and let AI do the thinking for you.

To Make the Great Decisions, Learn to Analyze Yourself First

Good decisions require you to think and analyze for yourself. Today we are moving so fast, we hardly take the time to look inward at ourselves, and that is not healthy for any good leader or decision maker. Through self-analysis you can see where you have knowledge and where you need help to make better decisions. Then you can tackle the project or problem that's on your plate.

Many successful people are able to analyze themselves and properly gauge their strengths and weaknesses. When you know your weaknesses, you can address them through study to gain knowledge that overcomes those weaknesses as well as knowing where to gather the resources you need in areas you are lacking.

While not everyone wants to know everything, to get answers and make good decisions you must be able to acquire the knowledge you need. Stock picker Peter Lynch, who I learned about during my senior year in college said, "Decision makers must be perfectionists." In talking about his field and expertise, he said, "The worst thing you can do is invest in companies you know nothing about."

So, how can you get started in mastering the art of decision-making for yourself? Start with these tried and true (but easily skipped if you rush) steps for sound analysis:

Make it a habit of writing down your criteria and expectations: Think of yourself as the great fictional detective, Sherlock Holmes. It's important that you gather all the necessary information to make a sound decision and be able to "see" it on paper. After you've collected enough data, focus on two or three key variables, prepare your case, and make a decision.

Learn to play devil's advocate with yourself: I love doing this. That's when you can act as a prosecutor and argue against yourself. Through the process, you'll gain more optimism toward where your decision is headed. You should also recognize if your decisions are really sound or if holes can be uncovered down the line. Lynch says it best, "The person who turns over the most rocks wins."

Get sound advice: Getting several opinions is important, but you need to be cautious of people who endorse their own personal views. You want to look for people who can be objective. Get multiple views and be prepared to act favorably when you identify that you have solid grounds on which to make your decision.

Keep an Open Mind: It's important to master this ability. The better you are at not blaming others for disagreeing with you, the better you'll be at decision-making. Why? Just consider that there are so many divisive people in our society, or so it seems, today. Many people you come into contact with might very quickly make snap judgments and that shows a lack of restraint as well as being quick-to-judge. Consider in our digital society; how many people have to walk back something they said, or apologize for reacting the way they did.

Restraint takes practice, but if you start to practice this skill, you'll make fewer mistakes and have fewer apologies. There's an old adage that is "spot on" which says: When I do right, no one ever remembers, when I do wrong, no one ever forgets." This is damn right and I'm sure you are nodding your head in agreement!

Keeping an open mind and allowing people to approach you with opinions that don't align with yours can save you from making costly errors in judgement.

Businessman Willard F. Rockwell had a process whereby he instructed his subordinates, peers, and even his superiors to find faults with his opinions. But disagreeing was not enough, they had to bring concrete evidence for their claims.

The fact is that in our hyper-driven economy we are making decisions faster, which can often lead to making more mistakes. We need to take time to do the best job the first time and not leave things to chance. Ask yourself, if you took another few days to make a decision, would it really create a problem, or are we simply trying to look good for someone, for ourselves, or for "the metrics"? You'll be surprised what people really need by "close of business" and what can wait until tomorrow morning.

Having strong decision-making processes is more important than ever. Keeping your pride in check and surrounding yourself with people who will tell you when you might be making a mistake is just as important. A track record of good "wins" does not mean you are guaranteed to make the best decision when the next major one comes your way. The last thing you need is to climb high up the ladder in your career only to lose sight of the important things, like taking time to make a smart decision.

Chapter 11

Finding Fulfillment in Life

A Guiding Principle for Fulfillment in Life

Do you often feel throughout the day that you are wasting your time? Ever feel like this when you come into the office on a Monday or leave on a Friday? You wouldn't be alone, according to Vilfredo Pareto, the Italian economist who created the Pareto Principle, also known as the 80/20 Principle. He states that a relatively small percentage of causes are those that lead to a large percentage of results. He announced his principle in 1897, after a study where he found that 20 percent of British subjects had 80 percent of the wealth.

Many studies have found that this 80/20 rule is common in all areas of society and life. Entrepreneur and consultant Richard Koch had written that 20 percent of the carpet in your home gets 80 percent of the wear. He also wrote that a small share of client's brings in 80 percent of a firm's profits. All this makes sense to me; because I've heard people say that 20 percent of any organization's staff does 80 percent of the work.

We can get granular with this concept, as it also applies to us individually. Yep, that means that 80 percent of what we do each day is a waste of time. Hard to swallow, huh? Basically, this means that a very small amount of activity or effort on our part every day yields a majority of our results. Ouch.

Now you may think: "not me, I get a lot done every day." But most of us walk away each day feeling pretty unfulfilled. Koch says, "Not enough time goes to do the work that matters most to us." The 80/20 Principle may suggest that we are all short of time, but Koch thinks the opposite. He thinks we have a lot of time. I also believe that we don't use our precious time each day, squandering it, by not doing what matters most, and which would make us fulfilled.

Here are my guiding tips to tilt the 80/20 Principle in your favor, to make you more focused and productive:

Start your day with thought and meditation: Instead of waking up and jumping out of bed or looking at your phone, get into a comfortable sitting position. Focus on what matters to you and what you really want to accomplish for the day. Don't be rushed in your thinking. Instead, visualize in your mind's eye—walk yourself through how you want to accomplish those important things. Remember, we talked about visualization earlier. Koch wrote, "Action is good only if it is focused action."

Focus your energy on what you like doing: "Logically speaking, those who achieve the most have to enjoy what they do," says Koch. It's just that simple. Make it a practice to think about this in a calm state every morning: you can create extraordinary value by doing what matters most, what gives you the most joy, what you feel most passionate about.

Think independently: No matter how large an organization you work for, it is critical for you to think independently to achieve success. Working in professional services, we would often say our business cards should be: "Vice President of my own desk." Even though I worked for a company, many of my client relationships were personally developed by me. My performance, creativity, and personal consultative interpretation were the factors that got me my clients. My business capabilities were what allowed me to provide expertise to a client, and that was what they bought—me, not the guy next to me at my company or another competitor. Koch wrote that the "Twenty percent who achieve the most either work for themselves or behave as if they do."

Eliminate low-value activities: Focus on the 20 percent of activities that give you 80 percent of your results. Work on eliminating the rest. You'll start to realize more accomplishments and ultimately what matters most: fulfillment in your life.

Learn to Recognize What Matters to You

Does this ever happen: you get ready to start your new day full of best intentions and focused on a set of tasks. You think to yourself: today "I'm going to get this and that accomplished—it's gonna be a great day!" You smile on your way to work and sing to your favorite music playing in your headphones.

You walk into work and you can just feel it. Reality is kicking in. Your coworkers are coming up to you with news about something unforeseen that went wrong. You pass your boss's office and she wave's you in—telling you to drop everything and jump on a new crisis. She is counting on you. While you spend your morning doing your part to put out the fire, new developments arise. You're trying to find time to keep all the balls in the air. After a long day, you walk out of the office—the last one on the team to leave and close the office. You leave feeling good that you didn't let any of those balls drop; you did a good job today – but exhausted. While cooking dinner and during your evening, you tell the people closest to you about your day. Then, when you put your head down for the night, you wonder what happened to the goals you set for yourself? Can you accomplish them tomorrow? You're not so sure. You realize you're now constantly working on putting out major fires you hadn't planned to be working on and this happens often in your life.

Does this sound all too familiar? It can happen in any aspect of life, whether you are in school, looking for a job, even looking for a house. You have a well-planned day ahead of you and it gets totally interrupted by all sorts of unexpected developments you must attend to. Is it possible to change this cycle of kicking your own wants and desires down the road when fires come, because let's face it, they always will? Yes, but you must take time to refocus and recalibrate the way you are currently operating. But you can do it.

Stephen Covey and Hyrum Smith, two men who specialize in personal effectiveness, say: "What people end up doing is the urgent, not the important." This applies to all levels of personnel, including managers and executive managers. These men state that more than 50 percent of manager's time is spent putting out fires and taking care of urgent matters.

You may now be wondering what the difference between urgent and important is; they sound the same. Keep an open mind and let me walk you through this. You'll realize they are most surely not. Let's break the two down.

Urgent matters are those necessities, such as crises and deadline-driven projects. They must be done or there will be consequences. Important matters are quite different—they are instrumental aspects of life, from school work to reports to major projects in business and in life. Doing what's important includes; planning, prevention, preparation, building relationships, as well as understanding values and real recreation. It's vital that you do not mistake what is important for what is truly urgent. Too many people make the mistake of thinking that every little thing is urgent, when it's not. By focusing and doing more of the important tasks in life, you reduce the number of issues that continuously arise each and every morning. This will require you to become more analytical. If you work on this, you'll see that less urgent matters arise and you'll realize that previously, at some point, you didn't keep your eye on the ball and you:

- Procrastinated
- Failed to plan appropriately
- Simply forgot to dot your i's and cross your t's
- Take on tasks that should not be assigned to you

Covey, in his seminars, uses a visual to bring home what matters most, and I really like it and think you will too: He uses a glass bowl, large rocks, small rocks, and sand. The large rocks represent what matters most in our lives, small rocks are lower priorities, and the sand is the lowest priorities. If you focus on and do the lowest priorities (picture him pouring the sand into the bowl) you can't get all the big and small rocks in. If, however, you focus on what matters most, putting the large rocks in first, then the small rocks, you can get the sand in too.

This is the crux of it all: people often do the lowest priority tasks first because they are easy or because they have not reflected on their priorities.

How can you understand what the lowest priorities are? "You've got to first know what you value," Hyrum Smith said. "Otherwise, you'll be heading all over the map." See, here's the thing: until you know what your values are, you won't know what to say no to. In not knowing your values, you'll say yes to too many things that you end up not really caring about. Yet you are obligated, by your own admission, to doing them. You find yourself constantly carrying out someone else's agenda. That is when your own goals are parked on the side of the road and you become disengaged.

It's easy to get lost today, not realizing that you haven't been focusing on what matters to you most. Through this loss of focus, you find a loss of satisfaction in your life. But with focus and taking the time to find what matters most to you, in rebalancing what is important and what is urgent, you can recalibrate your agenda and your life. You've got one life to live, so you want to live it and not someone else's agenda!

Here are a couple of points to ask yourself that will help you identify your values:

- What is your end goal? When you start your tasks, you must have your end goal in mind.
- Do you know where you are going right now? Learn what controls your time. Writing down what you do in the course of a day is an exercise to visualize if you've got time-wasters built into your schedule. Find them and eliminate them.

In going through this exercise, you'll find more happiness and hope for your future. You'll find a renewed sense of purpose. And you'll find yourself smiling more often.

Chapter 12

Focus on What Matters

How to Give Yourself More Time in Your Super Busy Daily Life

Time is money. We've all grown up hearing this expression. For many people, time is even more precious than money. It's about having opportunities to be with your family, doing the things you enjoy and helping those around you. Today, we have numerous time-saving and time management tools available at our disposal. So, how is it that so many of us feel like we can't find the time to get the things done that are important to us, or we feel like we are wasting time? One significant time waster is doing C-list priorities before we get to do the A-list priorities on our lists. Why do we do this? Because we are human, and the bottom-line answer is that many of us are subconsciously wired to want to do the easier things – the low hanging fruit, as they say.

Time wasters cause us to lose our focus and get off track on critical projects at work, in school, and quite frankly, life in general. Thus, we enter the downward spiral of feeling anxiety and pressure, missing deadlines, and producing work that is not our best nor worthy of our name. And, when it comes to our job, let's face it, we have little choice about producing: we've got to get the work done! Now, the only future outcome is what we will produce?

I've studied many time management techniques, including those in the books of Jeffrey Mayer, the author of *Time Management for Dummies* and

Zig Ziglar, author of *Over the Top*. From my studies of time management, I came up with my own simple six-step process that I discuss below:

1. **Clean your desk:** At jobs where it was part of our culture to leave the day with a clean desk (and a to-do list), I had some of the best producing days of my career thus far. Get into this new habit. Yes, it seems like a little pain the butt, but just try cleaning your desk each day for thirty days. This gives you a fresh start each day. You wouldn't want to sit down to eat at the table if the dirty dishes from last night, would you?

    See if this change makes a difference. I bet you'll find it a great way of organizing yourself.

2. **Toss it or File It.** Try this quick think three-decision process: as soon as a task pops into your head (or inbox), quickly forget it if it's not of importance or file it away for future reference. If it is important, add it to your master list of things to do—then refocus back to what you were doing. You can put a sticky on your monitor or a note on your phone and create this mantra: *TOSS IT/FILE IT/ADD TO-DO LIST.* This is a quick way of prioritizing tasks and saving time.

3. **Read an email only once:** Read and summarize news stories of relevance only once, if it's important, file them into a relevant folder and move on. Get into the habit of knowing what will drain your time. That is what the overload of our information age can do; it'll drain you and slow down your day if you read and re-read everything. It will seem as though everything can be relevant, but the truth is you can eliminate most of the information that shows up in your in-boxes and forget about it.

4. **Plan backward:** Another excellent habit is figuring out the outcome of the task you are working on, and planning a strategy to reach that outcome going backward. Write down all the details of how the outcome looks to you: this is a key to good planning. When you write it down, a few things happen when you do: you don't have to remember it, and the act of writing it down reinforces it in your mind. You will remember it better when you come across a conversation or read

something new, your brain will automatically align to your task if the information is relevant. Writing it down, also frees your mind from focusing on it – you know it's there on notepad, so you can focus your attention on getting back to important tasks.

5. **Don't just plan, start to act immediately:** Many people are good at planning. They spend endless hours planning their days and weeks, working on their online calendars and scheduling and rescheduling appointments. The harder part is taking action. Start the wheels of the bigger task right away; don't put it off for later. The reality of life is that it's best to do more complex tasks when you are freshest, earlier in the day when you have the most energy. As I mentioned earlier, most people use this time for C-list priorities. Remember back in school when you would put off the long and tedious paper you had to write, doing all the easy homework first? By the time you finished the easy stuff, you were probably too tired to focus on the complex paper.

   If this was you, and you still push off the more complex tasks, then you must reverse your strategy to do A-list priorities early, leaving the C-list priorities for the end of the day when you are worn down. This mental switch is going to be uncomfortable at first, but it's critical for success and the new high-powered you.

6. **Break projects down:** Breaking projects down into easy-to-handle pieces is vital to getting through them. That way you are not overwhelmed. Tackle the pieces separately and you'll find that you can produce a higher quality product, have less stress, and have time to review to see where you can improve before the deadline. It's a win-win-win.

To Find True Happiness Now, Think About the End of Your Life

Do you ever think about how hectic your life really is? How each year goes by faster and faster? Does it make you think about getting older, what you've accomplished, and what you'll be like when you retire? If you do, you're just like the rest of us. Throughout my management advisory career, I've also heard a lot of people talking about not getting enough done. It reminds me of *Tuesdays with Morrie*, the book about Morrie Schwartz who was dying from Lou Gehrig's disease. Author, Mitch Albom wrote about Morrie during the last few months before Morrie's death. In a series of conversations, they shed light on the importance of a proper focus in life.

Morrie came to terms with his disease; instead of obsessing over why it was unfair that he was dying and wallowing in his sadness, he looked at his slow death as a blessing. Putting things into perspective, he realized that unlike a quicker – or a sudden or even a tragic death, his fate allowed him to say goodbye to all his loved ones and friends as well as tie up all his loose ends. He also gave the world his final goodbye and teaching: "Study me in my slow and patient demise—learn with me," he said.

The advice Morris gave Mitch Albom and readers was this:

- Accept what you are able to do and what you are not able to do.
- Accept the past as past, without denying or discarding it.
- Learn to forgive yourself and to forgive others.
- Don't assume that it's ever too late to get involved (and interested) in life.

"Getting involved in life is made easier by first preparing for death," That way you can actually be more involved in your life while you're living it. As part of my self-motivated leader development system, I incorporate this teaching because we are all moving faster in our hyper-speed society and quite frankly, this faster pace is not always the better recipe for success. There are other reasons too, for example, personal engagement today is being eroded by our consumption of other people's opinions and thoughts that are can damage our personal psyche, which often are truly meaningless. For example, consider the social media platforms we integrate into our life, which are highly addictive. Today they are dominating our space, they bind us to our connections but can also strip us from concentrating on our thoughts before we react. They are consuming more of our time, and in some ways keep us from being present with our families, friends and from producing good work when we are at our jobs. Many argue this new constant consumption is stealing our precious personal time and even our employers time—but this is the new normal way of life.

Living life at a hyper pace does not really mean we are doing more and producing a lot. Think about it: we work more hours but feel less satisfied and many of us don't get paid for the extra hours either. How many times at work do you look at your coworkers and think, is that person even present? They look like "no one is home." Have you looked at your coworkers, staring at their phone instead of the PowerPoint, in a board meeting and wondered how many people are really paying attention? Why do so many of us walk around feeling that years go by but we are not accomplishing anything? This is because many of us are chasing someone else's agenda and dreams. We need to take time to recalibrate what we are doing in our lives. We need to find the real meaning. If you are simply chasing a paycheck, when your time comes, will the money you made be satisfactory? In this one precious life you have, by making money for something you many not really even care about, will you be able to say, "I'm happy with what I did in my life?" Food for thought.

So, what can we do? Glad you asked!

The good news is that, as the saying goes, it's never too late. If you are reading this, you can take a step forward into a whole new light. You can devote yourself to doing what gives you purpose, meaning, and fulfillment. Shall we begin?

Before even setting a new goal, it's important to ponder what your ultimate goal is. This is a process where we think about the finish line and work our way back. However, don't take so much time in this process that you keep stalling because you are not 100 percent sure what the "finish line" looks like. Although your finish line will change as you grow, year by year, you need a good idea of your end goal now. Then you can create your first new goal. Morrie explained that, "We put our values in the wrong things—and it leads to very disillusioned lives." He's right. I know in my past, I wasted years taking jobs that were not appropriate for my skill set instead of waiting for a more meaningful job. I wanted to be quickly employed again and start collecting a paycheck. A couple times, I essentially walked my career backward and I was very unhappy. A few times I took a job because I was promised a future role, one that would fit my skillset, but that job wasn't yet available. When I did this, the folks who hired me left the company shortly after I came on board and those promises were never fulfilled.

Still not sure how to start this exercise? Contemplate yourself at the end of your career or even at the end of your life. As you think about it, feel your emotions, too. What do you expect to have obtained in your life? Are you on the path to getting that? This contemplation will help you discover what's really important to you. You may find that the picture you paint looks good; you are definitely on the right path. But if the picture looks quite different, and you can see you've done little to reach your goals, or are not headed toward making them happen, well, you should strongly consider a change in direction. Write down what it would take for you to get there. It's key to write down all of the steps it would take for you to get there, too—don't cut corners. You need to see the full picture of what reaching your goal will look like because then you can plan a real timeline in achieving it. Then you can start taking the steps to making the change toward a more fulfilling life.

In doing this, you will, at a minimum, come out with a clearer picture of who you are and what you really care about. Setting new goals for your career and in life will give clarity and help you steer yourself toward doing what matters to you. You'll start to feel a new outlook towards life and hope of more meaningfulness. This alone will be exciting—and the possibilities of what is to come for you.

Dare to dream, and may your dreams come true.

Solid Goal Principles to Keep You & Your Team on Track

Have you ever heard of the saying: "It takes just a little chunk of time to make big impacts or outcomes?" Many people have quoted some version of this expression. Management consultant Ken Blanchard wrote the bestseller *One-minute Manager* many decades ago. Although the book was written a while ago, the many parallels of last century and much of business today, make it still relevant.

What Blanchard basically said is that people are the basis for the productivity of any company, and it's critical that they feel good at work if employers want to get the most out of human capital. His three important steps to making people feel good: Goal Setting, Praise, and Reprimands. I've studied a lot of management authors and speakers, and many older philosophies and techniques are actually just as relevant now when prescribed within the context of our hyper speed world.

Blanchard wrote that when you ask people to describe what they do at work - and then ask their manager, often you get two different descriptions. Why is this? Too often when you start a new job, your manager won't sit down and go over expectations or specifics. There's so much ambiguity! After some time on the job, you could list your role, as a combination of three different jobs – and at least one that you didn't sign up for either. To get more clarity, Blanchard wrote his "one-minute goal setting" ideas to clear up the ambiguity and create better communication. I've applied his principles to create my own management processes because I believe we all need more positive communication than ever before.

Goal setting for your employees, your team or whomever you lead. At some point in time, you may likely become an employer, a manager or a leader in some capacity. It is important to be prepared. As a leader you'll want to break down job descriptions or tasks into a few goals. Write out your version of the goals in 150 words or less. If it takes longer than one paragraph, you are not getting to the point. If it's too long you'll create ambiguity. Be focused.

Define good performance by clearly setting the goal and establishing what it looks like from your perspective. If they understand what you are looking for, you will more likely be on the same page. Discuss the goals with your employees, your team or whomever you are leading and gain a consensus of what it looks like from their perspective. That is, work on the goal until you've both agreed on a mutual performance target. Gaining a consensus and accountability is vital. Also take a moment to discuss what the possibilities of exceeding the goal could and would look like.

Through practicing this process, you'll become better at setting goals for other people, and by having strong communication while goal setting, they will feel more engaged in their work.

Give praise. As a leader, it will also be up to you to make sure people feel good and get the necessary mental uplift to keep the freight train of momentum moving toward and past the goal. You should let your team know that you'll be giving them feedback throughout the process. When you see people doing something positive, say so. Let them know right away. Don't wait a couple days. Tell them what they did, how it's going to help them, and the impact it will make.

Then let your team members respond—this is where you really must be listening rather than thinking of your response ahead of time. After listening, don't get into a discussion that will lead you off on tangents. Start on message and end on message. Let the praise sink in so team members continue with a positive attitude. Make a point of staying focused on the praise. Close with a handshake and a smile, looking the person in the eyes. (Praise should be given in both public and private.)

Giving reprimands. Just as with praise, try a reprimand when the problem occurs. Let people know upfront when something does not sit right. You want to give encouraging but corrective feedback when you see or hear an issue; that way team members or employees know you will be communicating and it's not a surprise. Tell people exactly what they did wrong. Also tell them exactly how it made you feel. It's important to be emotionally intelligent with your feedback and let them know where you are coming from. Therefore, it is key to explain the reasons why it is wrong.

Again, it's time for you to listen. Do not think about your next response. There may be a delayed silence, but you are not going to break it. Let the person collect their thoughts.

If there is a response, come back to your feedback and reiterate that you have faith in the person. Show encouragement, and tell them they are an important member of the team. If you see a problem with negative behavior add in the fact that such behavior is not good for the business. Close with a handshake and a smile, looking the person in the eyes. (Reprimands should be given only in private.)

Holding yourself accountable. Nobody is above making mistakes. When you realize that you've made one, own it. Get the team together if needed or meet one-on-one. Let the person or team know you've realized you made a mistake, and be specific in your acknowledgement. End with an apology and state that you're going to work to make sure it won't happen again.

Goal setting for yourself. Define your own goals. Write out goals in 150 words or less. If it takes longer than one paragraph, just as the advice above, you are not getting to the point. Today we simply operate faster and more direct. Define good performance by setting the goal and what it looks like from your perspective. It's important to note that this applies to leaders, coaches, anyone at any age – no one is above refining their own goals.

Read your goals often. Take time to look at goals twice a week: once during the week and then preferably once on the weekend. (Unless of course you work weekends, then on your days off).

This is where the rubber meets the road. Focus in a quiet place and give yourself thirty minutes. Look at your goals on paper.

Now ask yourself: Is your behavior this week in line with the goals you've written on paper? Be truthful. Then adjust your behaviors, if necessary, for the coming week. This process will help you become better at achieving your goals if they are truly important to you. You'll also be learning about yourself during this process.

Chapter 13

Dare to Show Your Creativity

Thoughts on People, Craziness and Creativity

Back in the 1800s, there was this guy named Percival Lowell who was a pretty successful business mathematician. That's one of the few things I can say flat out I could never be, is a mathematician. Aside from math, Lowell is best known for his belief in Martians: he claimed they created canals to transport water to Mars. Among his several published books, his best known was *Mars*, printed in 1895. Some scientists liked his ideas; some thought he was crazy. It's no different than the polarized world we live in today, especially where so many of us are divided with drastically different views.

Percival Lowell, crazy or not, also theorized a ninth planet in our solar system, one he felt sure was beyond Neptune. He searched for this new planet through his Lowell observatory, but passed away in 1916. Clyde Tombaugh, an amateur astronomer later discovered Pluto while working at the Lowell observatory. Regardless of whether Percival Lowell had some crazy ideas, if it weren't for his studies of Mars, Tombaugh would not have found Pluto. Lowell wrote, "One thing ... we can do, and that speedily: Look at the things from a standpoint raised above our local point of view; free our minds at least from the shackles that of necessity tether our bodies; recognize the possibility of others in the same light that we do the certainty of ourselves." Beautiful stuff, right?

I've always believed that my greatest gift is being able to thinking-outside-the-box. In fact, I said that on a final interview once. I had just shown an SVP my portfolio of awards and accolades for breaking quota production records. He then asked me, "What is the one thing you can bring to this position that makes you the difference maker?"

I replied that it was my ability to think outside the box and gave him some examples.

He paused and said he was shocked I didn't say a willingness to work hard.

I paused and then I said, "Well, I thought that was clear in presenting my portfolio. You can't have a track record of consistently breaking quotas if you don't work hard. The portfolio was a documented testament to my hard work. Saying that I work hard would be redundant. I didn't want to waste my response on that cliché answer, so I decided to highlight another attribute."

He abruptly thanked me and escorted me to the door as if I'd insulted him for presenting him with my rebuttal. Would I go back and change what I'd said? No, it was and still is a good answer and a great rebuttal.

What does this have to do with you? Learn to think outside the box. Many crazy ideas lead to awesome solutions. It's the crazy ideas that spark innovation. These days, it seems society is becoming too automated and robotic. Think of the calls you make to customer service centers. How do you feel when the person on the other line doesn't answer your question and reads from a script? When we talk to people who give programmed cookie-cutter responses it's as though we're talking to humans who are on autopilot. There's nobody at home on the other end.

Tom Peters wrote in his book on innovation: "Creativity is about jolting us out of our comfort zones." He was offered a project to work on a strategic examination for a rock/road asphalt company called Basalt Rock Co. Peters balked at the opportunity, but said he didn't have a choice. Later he wrote, "Turned out to be the best thing that happened to me." Peters said stepping out of his professional box reignited his creative flame to such a degree that he continued to put himself in ever more uncomfortable positions. He also booked speeches about topics where he had no expertise: it forced him into doing things that were different and uncomfortable.

Create an Acronym to Keep you Balanced

Being an avid reader, and having a creative streak, I started thinking of ways to get myself motivated in the morning. I'd put motivational quotes or stories on the walls of my apartment to read every day before heading to work. But I could never remember what I read; nothing stuck with me throughout the day. I needed something I could always remember and keep with me, especially when I started worrying about personal things that were taking me off track at work. I needed something that could get me focused quick and back on track.

I've always felt I never had enough time in my day to get everything I need to get done too. I would often wish I could freeze time at 3:00 pm, to get the day's work done before leaving for the day.

So, one day, I created my TIME acronym:

- *Tenacious*: Be persistent with getting my job done on time and within my expectations.
- *Integrity*: Be honest and upfront with the people I'm working with.
- *Motivation*: Stay motivated with the task at hand; I've only got X amount of time before my work day is done.
- *Empathy*: Be able to put myself in another's shoes. In recruiting I need to identify what other people are going through. Focusing on, and caring about what others are going through, is key for me.

TIME to get back to work! Time to focus on what I'm working on! TIME is precious, don't waste so much of it reviewing cat photos on Facebook or endlessly playing games on your iPhone!

I created my own acronym, and that helped me a lot when I was starting out. I stayed focused and hammered away at my tasks. I got to use a favorite word of mine to do so too. That's key in this lesson, because you want to remember that word all the time. Once I started using my acronym, it became special and a constant reminder that naturally motivated me to get back on track. Think of four or five attributes that are important to you, that you always want to have in mind, then take the first letters of them and form a word that you can use as an acronym. That can be your "word motivator." Then, when you get side tracked during the day, you will recall your acronym and follow your own recipe of attributes to get back on track.

With Creativity, You Too Can Be an Innovator

My first job was one of the best I ever had. Being in a dual role sales-oriented and recruitment advisory function, my creativity flowed because I was always thinking of new ideas, new ways to get new clients and helping find new solutions for those clients to get the best candidates. The firm I worked at was very entrepreneurial and I could bring my ideas, as creative and off-the-wall as they were, to my boss, who listened. I recall my boss singling me out on particular occasion for my off-the-wall ideas, when she gave a pep talk during an organizational low-productivity period, as a sign that I cared a lot about the success of the organization. I didn't think much of it personally, but it made a big impact on one of my employees and he told me so. That's what I never forgot – the impact it made on him and how important it was for me to express those off-the-wall-ideas – which today is highlighted as ideation-and-innovation. Today, there is a renewed interest in "employee voice" and "safe space" and when you have these your employees will be open to speaking like how I was – they will flourish and creativity will explode.

Pushing the boundaries at work is nothing new. We are constantly asked to raise the bar of our own individual performances. Today, if you don't raise the bar then you can find yourself on the out.

John Patterson founded a cash register company that eventually became NCR Corp. His story goes like this: Patterson asked one of his foremen to get a report on the work in his department. The foreman said: "I'm glad to report that we are 100 percent efficient, the men are loyal, and the best we can get. Our product is as perfect as can be made." Patterson asked, "Then you are perfectly satisfied?" The foreman said, "Yes, sir, I am." Patterson's response was, "All right, you are fired."

Of course, that was a long time ago and managers could say, do, and act like that then, but we are in a different age and time. But the point of Patterson never being satisfied with performance is similar to other leaders we recall that were like Patterson – for example, Steve Jobs.

You should never stop raising the bar for excellence. When you reach your set goals, it's time to set new ones. George Babish helped revive the YMCA, or the "Y," many decades ago. He did so with the process of *Imagineering*, a term invented by Disney.

Babish taught the process of Imagineering to YMCA employees, asking them to think outside the box and solve problems creatively. I was also using my creativity to solve problems in my sales roles—and acting on my creativity to produce innovative ideas and solutions that produced results. The key here is that when you apply your creativity with action, innovation happens.

Here are some ways to help turn your creativity into action and start innovating more frequently:

Speak up at meetings: When the boss, or any team leader, asks for ideas, speak up, even if the ideas seem crazy. Just do it and see where the conversation goes. You'll be recognized as the one who started conversations that led to possible solutions.

Do research: Got some crazy ideas? Find information to help support your ideas, do some research to provide supporting evidence. Then bring it to your manager.

Take risks: If you are a manager already, take risks with new ideas from your subordinates. This will show you are willing to try new ideas and that you care what your people think. If you are not a manager …. Then come up with some radical new ideas and don't be afraid to pitch them! You might even say to your manager, I'm not sure if this is a good idea right now, but I was thinking over the weekend and came up with a pretty interesting idea, can I run it by you? Chances are excellent that they be, at the very least, intrigued!

Listen to your customers: What are your customers saying? Ask (or survey) them for ideas. Then create new ideas that solve their problems or meet their needs.

Create new partnerships: Who are you not working with in your sales or marketing or advertising position (or whatever your position is called)? Can you build new relationships that are unconventional and can move your potential for creating new ideas forward? Can you bring in new technology opportunities that allow you and your company to do a process better, faster, or more efficient? Come up with experimental ideas that push your boundaries and take them to your manager. If possible, get funding and try things you've never done before.

Why You Should Believe in Yourself and Your Ideas

Do you think your company is an innovator? Do you feel that you work at a company that cares about innovation? Or maybe you think your company is innovative but your department is not. You're not alone if you think about these matters. Innovation is becoming more important to CEOs around the world; it should be essential to you, too. According to a PricewaterhouseCoopers (PwC) 2016 report on innovation, nearly three-quarters of CEOs regard innovation as at least equally important to operational effectiveness. That said, you can Google articles that report companies are simply not innovating fast enough.

Innovative companies have support at the highest levels. The same PwC report finds that CEOs see their role as a visionary. So, if CEOs see their roles as visionary and we understand that innovation happens when support comes from the top down, then it's clear that the top must drive the innovation process. I agree with top executives who state that a halfhearted attempt or limited commitment to a workforce's ability towards innovation will lead to inaction; the company won't be able to produce. That is one of the biggest reasons why we see annual reports of top executives, year after year, indicating innovation as a top priority. It's also why fewer companies report they are on target to meet their innovation goals.

Through my research and experience with technologies, I've seen that having too many people from the same group or department making all the creative decisions does not foster the best creative work group. You can learn this from DiSC selection concepts, numerous project methodologies and training programs, as well as from great visionary founders like Henry Ford.

Ford wrote, "All our new operations are always directed by men who have no previous knowledge of the subject and therefore have not had a chance to get on really familiar terms with the impossible. We call in technical experts wherever their help seems necessary, but no operation is ever directed by a technician." I always like having teams where half of the folks are not part my groups but rather from other departments with which I interact, or customers I support. No matter what field you are in, getting other people involved with no expertise in your field is an excellent way to get creative ideas flowing.

In the agency staffing world, I remember many times when a search was so daunting no one would work on it. A Fortune 100 customer reached out to us in 2010 — (at the height of the Great Recession when no companies were looking for new vendors to add)—sought our help in finding a global infrastructure director. We won the search because for months their preferred vendors sent no one good. After a few weeks, my whole team gave up and went back to the "pipeline fills." You know, the easy stuff to fill that you toss up and hope one sticks, "the low hanging fruit." I made a call directly to the HR director who told me the agencies she was working with were not responsive nor committed. After discussing what was lacking, I committed myself and my creativity.

After another month, even my own boss told me to move on—that it was a class Q (a very low priority fill) because of the complexity and lack of probability to make the hit. But I had a strong relationship with this HR director by then and she told me what I wanted to know on a regular basis, we developed a good bond, and she told me it was a priority for the company. So, I recognized the competing agencies had basically given up as did the others in my own firm, which means I've locked out my competition. That meant I basically had an exclusive search. A month later I landed the whale. My commission was two-and-a-half times a regular large placement. Result? Top producer for the month (also landed me in the top producers for the quarter again) in the tri-state area, and more importantly recognition from all my peers and my boss's boss too. The placement and my persistence to excellence was emailed out to all branches from Philadelphia to Boston, and employees I never met were sending me congratulatory emails for days. It's a good feeling and something that stays when you can make impact like that. The bottom line here is: creativity and determination equal mettle – and you build your personal armory to accomplish things others can't, won't and don't.

I'll leave you with a story about Dick Drew. In the 1920s, he was a 3M researcher who saw the need for tape that wouldn't remove fresh paint when it was peeled off. He worked on developing the tape for so long that the company president told him to stop working on the project and get on with his regular work. Drew stopped for a day. He then came up with a new idea and went back to the lab. After countless hours and hundreds of dollars spent on a paper machine, Drew invented masking tape. Now, Drew had defied the orders of the president and spent unauthorized money to buy the paper machine. But it taught the company an important lesson. For a long time after, 3M had the motto: "If you have the right person on the right project, and they are absolutely dedicated to finding the solution—leave them alone. Tolerate their initiative and trust them." What do you think Steve Jobs or Elon Musk would say about this story?

The Mind Mapping Method for Innovation

Whenever you read about successful people, oftentimes you read about something new they tried that separated them from the rest of the pack. Being innovative is many things: it's fun, creative, but it also means going against the grain. Many college programs today still don't teach curriculum about innovation; yet it's importance is paramount, so most folks end up learning about it through personal or work opportunities.

There is an interesting method called mind mapping for brainstorming, which is about developing your ideas and projects that you want to accomplish or create. For mind mapping, you need a few instructions up front: you'll need a large piece of paper to get the experience; (don't use a computer the first time you try this), multiple colors of pens, crayons, or markers and you need to give yourself the time to do this activity without worrying about anything else. So, if you are preoccupied with other things, or rushed with another project, learning to do mind mapping is not appropriate at that time. This process requires you to free your mind, be relaxed, and let your creative side come out—I suggest trying this and give yourself at least thirty minutes.

Get the biggest paper you can find: in mind mapping you want to start really big. Run down to your local crafts shop or Staples and get a piece of paper large enough to lay on the floor so you can be very expressive. If you can't do that, take regular printer paper and tape four pages together. Also, if you are going to run down to your local store, pick up a cheap pack of eight crayons or markers, or borrow them from the kids. The key is to use colors to let creativity surface: one or two pens is not going to cut it. Now write or draw your idea, your main theme, or an image of what you want to accomplish.

By the way, I get it. None of us use paper to do our work anymore, we do everything on a computer. But there is something to this creative project that requires you to think "larger than your laptop or tablet." You need to try the paper mind mapping for yourself at least once. Then you can use software and do it on your computer. If you are in extreme pain at the thought of this, do a reality check. I already gave you the suggestion above to tape a few pieces together if necessary. If nothing else, you can spread out a few pieces of paper on your kitchen table and just keep them next to each other. The point is to do this exercise at least once in this original way.

Now, the brain works best in five-to-seven-minute bursts, according to Joyce Wycoff, owner of an innovation company—and she is not the only one to say it.

In mind mapping, we are trying to come up with as many ideas as possible within a five-to-seven-minute timeframe. Think of mind mapping as an explosion of ideas that you grab and put down as fast as possible. Nothing is incorrect. The key is the fast pace of thinking here.

Set your phone timer.

Get ready and go! Remember, even if it doesn't make sense, just capture your ideas and put them down on the paper. If random thoughts appear, write them down to get them out of your mind. The concept is that if you don't and you hold onto them, your mind will take up precious resources to remember them, so store them in order to recall them later. Get everything out of your head and onto the paper, even just a word so you can see it later and rapidly get back to your central theme.

There's no time to stop to judge your thoughts. In this mind mapping exercise, it's essential to write down whatever you think of in whatever color you want. Let your mind go freely where it wants. Don't judge.

The formation: The goal is to have your central theme in the middle with lines leading to other ideas and then for those ideas to sprout more branches. As your ideas spring other ideas, draw lines that connect them. Keep going and don't stop thinking. Keep branching out and using different colors for new ideas.

As structure happens, let it. When natural connections happen, and they may, allow them to show up either close to, or connected to each other. But don't take time organizing, let it happen spontaneously. As ideas appear that are totally different, capture them on the opposite side of the paper. You will organize your ideas when you are done.

When your time is up, look at what you did, then analyze it and organize it. Take the rest of the twenty-three minutes for this analysis and organization, then study your results.

Believe in Yourself and Be Brave Enough to Innovate

Remember the movie *The Matrix* where Morpheus offers Neo the red pill or the blue pill? Take the safe route or the one that can change your life—but, remember, there's no going back.

In a story about Jack Matson, the reader (you in this situation), is asked if there were a thousand pills and one was lethal, how much money would it take for you to take one and test your luck? That isn't a game I'd play—and I also don't equate that gamble with being worthy of calculating risk to innovate or belief in yourself-as-lucky. But there is no question that when innovating you must take some risks.

As you have read through this book you've learned that taking calculated risks and failing, this is part of being creative and innovative. No one expects that they will wake up and create a billion-dollar business without taking some risks. Matson, who is a multi-patent holder and innovation researcher said, "Educating yourself about the subject matter, performing a cost-benefit analysis and picturing the rewards of successful risks" is what you must do to innovate. He also said, "Innovation is the process used to create novelty".

But why don't we take more risk and why don't more of us innovate? Because, it's not easy to do. After all, being a risk taker and taking the road less traveled often means going against norms. Fear is a big part of this. Fear of the unknown, fear of being ridiculed, fear of what people will think of your ideas, fear of losing your title or your job and more. History is full of great people who were ridiculed and cast out for their innovative ideas while they were alive. But, that was then and this is now.

There are things you can do to help you start being more innovative:

Start easy, with creativity tasks: You don't need to be anxious about starting this process. Start by making your life more fun. Plan a different route one day next week to work and leave twenty minutes early. Take a class that is not in your direct field of work, but in an adjacent field. (Think about some of your colleagues, the ones who do some pretty cool stuff that you admire – it can motivate you to take a class in that field) One of the things I do is I write things down on my white board and color coordinate by stage of completion and by category. Go to the library and check out some new magazines. I enjoy car racing but before 2016, I had never gone to a race; so that year I went to three races in different cities, so I got to visit new places at the same time.

Get your ideas out of your head: I have been recording my ideas since I graduated college. Back in the day I had a hand-held mini tape recorder. Now of course, I just use my phone. Record your ideas and review them every weekend, transfer your ideas to a Word document and create a folder—which is what I do. Get into this habit and you'll never go back, it's awesome how many ideas will start flowing through you.

Failure is part of the journey—don't be afraid to fail: The folks who say failure is not an option might be saying this as a motivational slogan. I heard that slogan many times in my younger days, when I was in sales: "Failure is not only an option"! It sounds good but it doesn't fit in the real world. The truth is, it's a part of the process that leads to successful innovation. Trial and error are one of the most significant ways in which we learn. Error means failed attempts – you learn from such errors and keep on going. Look at any great inventor. Do you think Edison invented the first commercially practical incandescent light on the first try? Did the Wright Brothers get the first plane off the ground?

Always be innovating: If you do, soon enough you'll realize that you are thinking differently all the time. That's good, don't turn that thinking off or try stopping yourself from thinking in an innovative way. It's great when you're thinking in a creative and innovative way. In fact, I enjoy helping my friends by playing in the "devil's advocate" mode. I think it helps me, and them, consider all options; I safeguard myself from jumping into a decision when I consider multiple options.

Don't let a funk get you down: I remember my second year in agency recruiting, it was Q4 and I hadn't made a placement in months. This was highly unusual for me, and I remember sitting in my boss's office and saying something to the extent of, "I think maybe I'm washed up. I'm no good anymore."

She spent over an hour talking to me about her experiences and hammering into my head that I had hit a bump on the road that would pass. She made me repeat it a few times before getting out. What happened next? Over the next few years, I broke about six quota records, to the point I was just trying to break my own ones. At one point I was the number one producer for eleven straight months. So yeah, let me tell you—funks do come but they will definitely go—stay the course.

Chapter 14

Developing the Art of Communication

Use Assertive Communication to Stand Out at Work

Management coach Sharon Bower tells a story about how in high school she felt confident about winning a tournament for her debate team—but lost. From that point on she focused on not just her strategy but other people as well. She wrote the book *The Assertive Advantage* in which she says, "Assertive communicators identify with what their audience wants to hear —and they can predict how these people will react."

Bower went on to say that if you're an assertive communicator, you get things done while getting along with others." She's right. My entire career in strategic talent acquisition is based on getting multiple people and parties on the same page. If I can't, then people don't get hired – and I fail at my job. In today's changing workplace, it's critical to get along with others to get your own job done. People who don't work well with others won't be able to work well in their companies for long.

The reality is that you're going have to work with people you wouldn't socialize with outside of work. That said, in the workplace, we all get paid to work with each other. Therefore, to help you succeed, I've designed these points below to create a strategy that will keep "good communications with people" at the top of your mind:

Use focused positive language: Practice verbalizing positive expressions at work with peers, administrative staff, leadership and especially clients.

For example, focus on saying people's names when you talk to them. People remember when you use their name; you are connecting to them and it makes them feel good. When giving positive feedback try, "Mike, I really like the way you created that PowerPoint" instead of, "That PowerPoint was done well." You are expressing your personal liking and directing it to a person specifically. It's a small change, but it makes a big difference. Just think of how many positive remarks you'll make in a year when focusing on this change. You will enhance your leadership skills and people will like you more.

Be Observant: We are living in a pretty charged up state-of-life and work today. Make a habit of observing other people's emotions through body language, facial expressions, and vocal tones—these clues can tell you about their mood and what they're thinking. Practice making comments that acknowledge someone's mannerisms, such as, "I noticed you seemed at ease after the V.P. made those positive comments about your presentation today." Learning to be more "in tune" with other people's emotions will help you bring people around to your points of view, and you'll be viewed as someone with whom people can connect.

Learn to disagree amicably: It's easy for people to say the wrong things today and not be able to take it back since we communicate in so many forms. To play it safe, try disagreeing in a less critical way. Instead of saying, "I don't agree with you" or "I don't see how that can work," you could say, "I'm not yet sure if I understand how that will work." The difference is subtle, but the approach opens the possibility that if they can explain it better, you may see their point of view more clearly. Being less confrontational is important in today's sensitive workplace environment.

Clarify and confirm: Being in a global economy means talking to people from all over the world to get projects done. It's more important than ever to make sure you understand instructions properly. Assertive people know this and ask for clarification by saying, "I just want to make sure I heard you correctly"—and then repeat what was said.

Or "I know you have to go, but let me just repeat your instructions so I'm clear and don't make a mistake."

Being assertive is especially helpful when a request seems odd or unreasonable. Practice with a positive opening to your inquiry and then clarify, as in, "I want to make sure I do a good job on your request, but wouldn't my doing this task be duplicating the work done by Jennifer, or am I mistaken?"

Be Persistent: Assertive folks also know that when someone promises something, they follow up. So, don't let someone who owes you something drop off because they've "just been so busy." That will never change. Everyone is "always just so busy." When someone owes you something, it's okay to persist by giving little reminders like, "Hey there, not sure if you remembered but you promised to show me that new app and help me install it—can we get that on the calendar for this month?"

Learn to Work with Difficult People

Dealing with difficult people is probably one of the toughest things we do in life. It's not easy to go to work in an environment where you know you'll soon be in the presence of someone who complains endlessly or lowers team morale—or someone who is the polar opposite of you and your beliefs.

Remember, you can't change difficult people—or people in general— but you can communicate with those people in a way that gets your point across while giving them ideas to consider that might help them change their own behavior.

But the key is for you to stay relaxed and remain calm and mindful, which is easier said than done, isn't it? Here are some methods to help you build a strategy that can help you in your career journey.

Emulation throwback: You have your agenda, but you're dealing with difficult people and you want them to see things your way. Here you must give a little praise and let them know what you want from them. For example, you might say; "In this department we all try not to react too quickly, we take time to absorb what other people say and then look for solutions. I know you're a smart person so I don't think you'll have any trouble fitting in."

Intentional praise: In sales, once you become a leader, you'll certainly want to see your people perform at higher levels. You often have to set expectations. In setting new expectations don't focus on the past, old failures or complaints. Instead, set the goal or the achievement in a straightforward way. For example, "This quarter I'd like to see you double your sales proposals." Then follow up with praise, as in the above method, by saying, "You are a bright person in this department, I know you can do it."

First person language: When you are in a discussion, make it a practice to talk about how you see things. For example, "From what I'm seeing it looks like..." or "The way I saw what unfolded was...." According to experts, this phrasing tells the difficult person you're expressing *your* truth rather than claiming it to be "the absolute truth," or condemning their truth.

Focus on behavior, not people: When you want to correct a person's behavior it's important to focus on the perceived actions of the person and not the person. Saying something like, "John what you did was inappropriate" focuses on John. Instead, say the same thing in a way that stresses the behavior, such as, "Doing the act of _____ could be perceived by someone, especially in our heightened state of sensitivity today, that you didn't care. But John, we know that's not you. Can you see how someone could perceive it that way?"

Navigate tighter meetings: Today we all must be sensitive to everyone's input and participation. Meetings, however, can still go off on tangents and people often dominate the time by blaming others or complaining about something. In the end nothing gets accomplished.

If you are leading the meeting, it's okay to interrupt and steer the meeting back on topic. The key is to remain calm and repeat the person's name until you get their attention. If they raise their voice, you can do so as well, but you don't have to. Don't be aggressive and don't draw attention to that person—instead politely steer the conversation back to the purpose of the meeting. Even when you're not leading a meeting, you can wait until you have the floor and ask, "can we please try to stay on the topic?" You might then add, "I know we all have very busy schedules and don't want to waste this time." **Motivate positive change:** When talking to someone about their behavior, make sure to focus and be specific. Explain the "why" a person's behavior is not serving them well, so they can see the impact it has on them. Then present alternatives but leave the change in their court. Let them know that the change they pick can have a positive impact for them.

Make sure your strategies incorporate these tips:

Give options. Give options and then allow the person to choose. When asking for a behavioral change, suggest a few options but leave it up to the person to select the positive change. This gives the person accountability and the ability to take credit for their choice to make a change.

Don't be rigid. Be flexible and open to possible scenarios. Listen to other people's point of view. You can then craft solutions to meet the change.

Honesty is the best policy. Being honest is important, but it's also important to tell the truth in a way that does not put egg all over someone's face. Show the person they still have good qualities and contributions; when you do this, you may coax out the change you want to see.

Making a good first impression

We all know that making a good first impression is essential. In business, it's critical. In fact, a bad first impression might end a relationship before the relationship begins. Knowing that making a good first impression is so important; we also can get nervous. We may even panic – but that's okay—you should know, we all go through it.

Why is a first impression so important? Study after study shows that humans interpret the behavior of others in a way that correlates and is consistent with the initial viewpoint or experience, we have with that person. So, if you make a good impression and solid follow through, it will leave a lasting positive feeling. But if you make a bad first impression, it becomes a tough uphill battle from that point forward. As David Lieberman, a behavioral researcher wrote, "Everything we see and hear afterward gets filtered through our initial opinion."

In an experiment involving a person who was to be a college lecturer, the researchers presented two descriptions:

A. Cold person, industrious, critical, practical, and determined.
B. Warm person, industrious, critical, practical, and determined.

In the study, one group of students received list A and the other list B. The students who read list A considered the words "critical" and "determined" to be associated with negatives, while the students given list B viewed all the terms in a positive way. The only difference here was the opening words of the description, yet those words changed how students perceived the rest of the description.

Now that we know what happens with the first impression and why it's so important, we can prepare ourselves to make the best and most positive impressions we can. It doesn't have to be nerve racking; in fact, it's easier than you might think, but practicing anything, makes you better. And today, when everyone is so busy and uses that as a continuous reason for making excuses, you can shine and separate yourself from your peers.

Smile: I know what you are thinking—Duh, everyone does this! But do they? Lieberman says, "It may seem obvious, but most people forget to smile." Slight nods or a half smile don't count either—they have little effect compared to a full and genuine smile. Studies show that smiling does four powerful things: It conveys confidence, happiness, enthusiasm, and most importantly acceptance. I am adding another powerful aspect, it helps you internally calm down; it's a stress reducer. Want to put it to the test? Take an hour or two and count how many people you encounter who are not smiling or look away when you make eye contact.

Speaking in first person with positive words: Work on your language when introducing yourself and in giving praise by using more first-person language. For example, instead of saying, "It's nice to meet you" say "I'm really happy to meet you." This minor difference puts an emphasis on your positive reaction to the person. Also, make sure your resume is written with positive words that present you in the best light—conveying your best attributes.

Focus on the other person's interests: It's been said that President Teddy Roosevelt would amaze people because he would find out about the other person's interest's and bring them up when he met them. Most successful salespeople know how important this can be to their success. I've been doing this my whole career—in the agency staffing business and especially before LinkedIn, it was critical for me to convey the "hot buttons" about the hiring manager to my candidates. Today with social media, you'd think more folks would be prepared, but many people still don't do it. Learn about the people you are about to meet, where they worked, attended school, and their hobbies. It will help you make a much more lasting impression in a sea of people who don't know how to do this.

Make the other person's needs matter: When you are talking to someone, focus the time on how you can help that person. If you do, you'll see a more genuine interest reciprocated towards you. Win-win.

Use humor: I see this as a hallmark of working successfully with other people, especially when meeting people for the first time. Because I come from a sales-oriented recruiting background, if I could meet someone for the first time and talk about their hot buttons, then add some humor and get them to smile and laugh, I always knew it was going to be a good conversation.

Getting people to laugh breaks down barriers, changes the mood, and cuts the tension in a meeting. When people brought up Ronald Reagan's age, he would say he was best friends with Abraham Lincoln and that his social security number was 1. Self-deprecating humor is especially effective because it allows you to confront issues about you and your mannerisms, and it reflects a much-admired human attribute, humility—and we all love humble people. Be careful, however, humor must be appropriate to the situation and neither insulting or in bad taste. And don't assume you know things about individuals based on what you read or hear either. It's better to joke about something that is common ground, which could be about the traffic jam you were stuck in, something funny you saw on the trip over (or in the media) or a non-controversial topic of general interest.

Learning to Speak to Your Audience Takes Practice and Effort

Developing the art of communications is a very tough thing to master whether it is writing, spoken or even nonverbal communications. Today, we are living in the most multi-discipline, multi-dimensional communications world ever.

The key to having strong and successful communications is maintaining control and command over the people you speak to and how you speak. It is an art and you have to display self confidence in the way you present yourself and communicate. You also have to be careful and conscious about what you say and how you say it. Unfortunately, sometimes when we try to say the right things, we just don't say it in a way that everyone processes it the way we expect, but we still have to try.

So how do great speakers do it? Two fundamentals are knowing when you're losing your audience and of course what to do about it. It's important to know that your audience is going to start judging you from the moment you start to speak so I just want you to keep that in mind.

Some of the most talented people that speak today are stand-up comics; they not only have the self-confidence to speak in front of many people (which is never easy) but they are able to be vulnerable, and lay it all out there to get laughs. In fact, some of the most talented people speaking today are comedians, such as Kevin Hart who is a very skilled and successful.

Like other comics, Kevin Hart gets his audience focused and involved by asking them questions and then he'll go into describing something funny - this is about audience participation, even though they don't answer his rhetorical questions. For you, it may be more pressing questions you will answer in a conference room. Asking questions creates dialogue, so talking to your audience can start by asking them questions about whatever your topic may be. This way, you should know that they will get the answer and even if they don't, you will provide it. This should be something they will typically agree with or are at least interested in hearing about.

Another key part of communication is repetition. This is actually a very classic tool that many great orators throughout time have used; Martin Luther King used the now famous words "I have a dream," eight times in his speech.

Hart always talks about his children as a theme in his comedy, and he continues to repeat his themes. When you are speaking and want your audience to remember what it is you want them to know, you should pepper your presentation with some repetition.

Another great tool to use when communicating is storytelling. Kevin Hart, is a very strong storyteller, and this helps him put his audience right in the moment with him. Like other storytellers, Hart uses vivid details and imagery to make you actually see it in "your mind's eye", as I call it, and when you can do that, you can make your stories come to life. This makes them memorable and, in our world today, where we are bombarded with information, will make your presentation really stand out.

While you should consider the ideas I've presented above, you'll also want to keep in mind these key points below which are tell-tale signs you are losing your audience. If you're in a conference room and you're talking to your audience and asking questions, but you have continued silence that's a problem which means you're not connecting with your people and they are not able to quickly come up with responses - or they're not following you.

If you look around and you see people checking their phone or not making eye-contact it could mean they are disengaged or they are engaged, but again, they're not following you.

When you're speaking, do you see that people have their arms crossed tightly or do they have a more relaxed position? Notice whether there is open or closed body language. While you're speaking you want to keep an eye out for this. If it's closed body language, you may need to engage them more, and even lighten the tone to get them to open up more to your presentation.

If you hear people whispering or trying to talk to somebody else next to them while you're speaking, that could mean they are disengaged and you're losing their attention. Again, engage them; consider incorporating your ability to "on-the-fly" ask questions when that happens.

Ultimately the art of communications, especially public speaking in front of many people, is one of the hardest things any of us will have to learn. I remember hearing in college that one of the top three things most people fear is having to speak in front of a large audience. Well, that was then, and it's true today and I bet it'll be true tomorrow. My point is that you should not be so hard on yourself, the vast majority of us are scared and don't want to attempt public speaking, but knowing all this you are already ahead of the curve. Communication takes time to develop – for some it'll come easier but for most of us it'll be tougher. And finally, like all things in life practice makes perfect. Kevin Hart spent years honing his craft. In fact, it did not go well at first when he started out as Lil Kev. He was booed off the stage often, but he was confident that he had something funny to say, and over time he honed his material, practiced it as often as possible and eventually started winning comedy competitions, on his way to becoming both a world-famous comedian and movie star.

Learning the Art of Listening

In the workplace, at school or in social interactions, listening skills are critical. But many of us don't take the time to practice, nor are we really good listeners. In fact, it's a skill that can be taken for granted because many of us think we are good listeners. Think of the people with whom you are most often with: are they people you identify as having poor communication or listening skills? Being a poor communicator is a problem in any area of life today.

Mastering the art of listening is one of the most effective skills you can have in life. Keep in mind, listening doesn't just mean hearing other people's words, it means focusing on what message they are trying to convey, focusing on what they say, and determining their intent. Why are they telling you something? In other words, listening means absorbing what is being said.

Choose a quiet place. When having a one-on-one conversation with someone, pick a place free from noise, phones, and other distractions. You don't want interruptions nor a place cluttered with other stuff going on. You want to pick a place where you can focus, and let the speaker relax and be able to talk freely. Remember to put your phone away and on silent —do not check anything on it for the time you are in this conversation with the other person.

Practice good posture: Posture may not seem like much, but it matters. Remember, you don't know what you look like, but if you are slouching or are fidgeting it conveys a sense of inattentiveness. Practice facing the other person squarely and try not to cross your arms with a non-stressful facial expression—in other words, stop thinking of what else you have going on. Show an open and inviting facial expression with a slight smile.

Don't give cookie cutter responses: Make sure you are really listening so you don't give a standard "That's interesting" or "Is that right?" response. Be original and present in the conversation, otherwise you can be perceived as not having really listened. In being present and authentic, make sure not to interrupt, while at the same time, showing that you are paying attention by nodding, and or smiling when you agree and occasionally asking a question for more specific clarification.

Show real interest: Maintain eye contact with the speaker. Don't fidget around with things or look around or down at your phone. Although it seems like a no-brainer, since we are constantly multi-tasking it's easy to forget, so, keep this top of mind.

Paraphrase and clarify: Restate in your own words the key points are that the speaker is making. This is very important in the dialogue so that your counterpart knows you've been paying attention, and by reiterating what's been said, you are making sure you received the correct information. You can use openings like, "What I'm hearing you say is..." or "How you felt during this is..." or "Essentially what happened is..." You can also ask questions like, "I want to make sure I understand what happened, is this [the situation] what you are trying to say?"

Ask real questions: If you are running a project or a team, and a colleague isn't pulling his or her weight, or if someone comes to you with a situation, don't ask general or standard questions like "Do you need some help?" If the person didn't need help, they wouldn't have come to you. Ask more specific questions that pertain to the person's situation, such as, "What steps do you think you can take based on this scenario that will give you the best outcomes?" Asking this kind of question is more specific, it keeps you actively engaged and shows your genuine interest in helping the other person. Even if you can't help, it shows you're a strong sounding board and a person that can be counted on to share their concerns.

Stay cool in the conversation: Anger can destroy the conversation. It will distort the perceptions of the conversation; it will not allow you to remember the facts of what was being conveyed and erodes the promotion of an honest communication. If you feel yourself getting angry, change the subject or politely excuse yourself from the conversation for a moment, cool down and then come right back.

Listen objectively: A critical feature to work on is listening objectively. Practice not judging the other person but really hearing their point of view. Otherwise, you can't listen with genuine openness nor think critically. With an open mind you can think of options and weigh in by offering your thoughts.

Assume your action. The final part of being a responsible listener is to act on what you've heard. Summarize what has been discussed and tell the person what action you recommend and what you can do to help them if you can. Follow up and keep the person informed too—do not drop off. If you don't follow up, that person may feel as though the whole conversation was a wasted and a manipulative exercise.

Chapter 15

Honesty and Ethics

Good Ethics Matter — and Will Pay off

What's wrong with a little lying and stealing? A little cheating doesn't hurt anyone, now does it? If you think this way, you couldn't be more wrong. Not only do these actions affect your own moral fiber and conscious, but unethical behavior always leaves someone holding the "bag of blame." Such conduct in the business world, can result in heavy fines, loss of reputation, bad press globally (think social media) and even lead to a company's demise.

Chances are good that your honesty will be tested many times on the job during your career. Winthrop Swenson, a former deputy general for the U.S. Sentencing Commission wrote many years ago, "Inside the (dishonest) organization, people are prodded, pushed and incentivized to do wrong things." We've seen this happen time and again in countless stories that make the daily headlines. Just look at the story from 2017 in which Wells Fargo created fake customer accounts—how crazy was that? It's the stuff that makes Hollywood wonder, "Can we compete with the real news?" A company mantra of, "I don't care how you do it, just get it done" has led many employees to do things against their ethical standards—and led them to ruin their own careers.

People, and companies, have been finding ways of being dishonest for ages. But good companies, and good people, believe that honesty pays off. Having integrity is a great competitive weapon in your arsenal, and besides, the downside is far greater than having ethics violations put forth against you.

By simply having a code of ethics in place, companies and individuals can define and maintain standards of positive ethical behavior and reduce their exposure to ethical violations by up to 99 percent. Good business ethics and having a strong sense of integrity work well: one hand washes the other and you need both. As an individual, you'll need both to be credible with your subordinates, peers, superiors, vendors, and customers. You'll build a positive reputation over time and be known as someone who stands for what is right, and tells the truth. Here's the beautiful thing about ethics: when honesty is a motivating enabler for uncovering a problem, you can be the person in charge of finding the solution. This also frees your mind from having toxic moral dilemmas. Why would you want all that mental anguish anyways? Honesty allows you to have a good reputation, gain a leadership position, and boosts your career in a variety of ways, while opening doors.

Being honest, and ethical gains you more respect than being a liar. It also saves you a lot of time and effort thinking up lies and backing them up with more lies. Just think about what you know today and what is going on around you—all of that affects you. Who do you consider liars and who is telling the truth? You probably have less respect for the liars.

You might be wondering what it takes to develop a good code of ethics. You're not alone. Just because you have good values, though, doesn't mean you'll be using them in your future endeavors. For some of us it takes work to do the right thing—but the good news is you can be ethical and successful at whatever you do in business and in life.

There are many organizations, and religious institutions that can help you better understand how to be more ethical in all aspects of life. You can also find strong ethical principals in people that you know and trust.

In this day and age, it's also important that you are careful not to let technology turn you into an unethical person. Even though we've been using technology to communicate for decades now, people still think that telling a fib or a little white lie online, in a blog post or even in an email, doesn't count. Some people find that it's easier to lie using technology rather than in a face-to-face situation. But the bottom line is that lying can be just as harmful online as it is in person.

We also give ourselves passes by convincing ourselves that there are reasons why it's okay to lie to meet our business, or personal obligations. Folks think that because they have major financial obligations like mortgages or car payments due, that it's okay to lie here and there or cut corners. You must make the choice of either growing ethically as a person or not — and if you choose not to, you will be hurting yourself in the long run; yes, you will be tarnishing the reputation of the person you'll see every day in the mirror.

The good news is that you can make a choice. Having good ethics is becoming more fashionable these days. In fact, many business people are talking about transparency which is based on being ethical. You can, and should, practice transparency and be proud to have good strong ethics. If you don't feel like your company is on the right path, you have an opportunity to champion a new code of ethics. This means your company can follow a better (more ethical) set of guidelines.

Are you getting pressure to engage in unethical activities? Does it feel like your company is taking advantage of your moral fabric? I've got more good news— a lot of companies are hiring people with a high moral fabric, good ethics, and a strong personal character. As the old Monster. com commercial used to say, "There's a better job out there."

Good People Finish at the Top

Ever heard the old saying "good guys finish last?" Well, whether you have or not, it is exactly that—an old saying. And it might as well stay in the past. Because good people are often very successful. Studies have long shown that kind people are good at their jobs and they attribute their success on the job with being kind.

That's not all. Today, more than ever, everybody is watching communications. Plenty of research on corporate hiring has been done and the evidence is clear that most managers notice employee behavior and appreciate when an employee exemplifies thoughtfulness and helpfulness in the workplace. Such behavior also comes into consideration when it's time for a raise or a staff promotion.

The Soft Skills: Just as Important, if not more than the Hard Skills

When it comes to what management has focused on during most of this century, we in talent acquisition know the priorities have been on the technical and hard skills, and not so much the soft skills – until you get to higher executive levels. This has been a mistake and entering out of the pandemic, its being realized. But what are the soft skills? Simply put, they are the human attributes. A term that I like is "good corporate citizenship behavior". This means that a person takes on assumed responsibility for those around him/her in the workplace while doing their job. Chances are excellent you will not see this on a job description. It's very hard to measure the value of soft skills.

You may have heard someone say "that person is a role model of this organization..." This means doing what they should do and then some – going the extra mile, if you will. The good news is that even if you've never thought about this or feel that you lack this attribute, it can be learned and practiced.

In building a good personal strategy, pick three of the attributes below (or soft skills) and focus on developing them for a specific period of time, (say three-to-six months). Then focus on the others too. As you practice them in your workplace, make notes of how you are progressing, and what reactions you're receiving. Make this a fun process to help you achieve "good corporate citizenship" – and over time, watch the wonderful things that happen for you at work.

Altruism: This essentially means being concerned about others. You can display altruism by simply taking the time to help a coworker through something they are working on— and asking for nothing in return. For example, helping an introverted colleague become more comfortable speaking to executives on marketing calls.

Courtesy: This is important; it's about taking the time and showing respect for other people. In business this might mean something as simple as alerting co-workers that you are about to do something that could affect them in some way. For example, telling a colleague you're going to propose something to a client that may affect their department or adding software that might interrupt their work for a couple of minutes.

Civic virtue: This is when you are willing to do the right thing even when it's unpopular. Speaking up about something that is not right. Simply put, standing up and doing the right thing.

Peacemaking: The ability to resolve conflict within a workplace is a strong attribute and gets noticed at the top of soft skills when leadership promotion is being brought up.

Sportsmanship: This is the ability to take on responsibilities, even though it's not in your job description. It also means letting go of some responsibilities for whatever the reason is – and doing it without complaining.

Cheerleading: This involves going out of your way to cheer for a colleague or group in their endeavors. Encouragement. Refocusing your teammates. Being a motivator and an inspiring coworker.

Patience: When you have this quality, you show tolerance for people, even when they have caused trouble. The ability to be patient and not get angry is important in the workplace.

At the end of the day, being a good corporate citizen is about engagement in the workplace, doing the right things, taking the time to care about, and help, others. Going above and beyond. Today, just as it was when I graduated college twenty years ago, the math for most company's workforce is the same. The Pareto Principle states that "80 percent of employees fizzle and 20 percent of employees sizzle". Many factors determine how a person gets selected for a promotion, but this lesson will definitely be a strong ally as you navigate your career and strive for business success and promotions.

Honesty is the Foundation for Business Success

Do you like to do business with people that seem shady or people who lie? Nobody does. Honesty, often referred to as transparency, has been a cornerstone for being respected and admired in business. It doesn't matter what the profession is either, imagine if a doctor or lawyer was found to have been doing shady business? Would you use their services? In the professional services and corporate worlds too, it is paramount that a client must be able to trust the professionals with whom they are working.

Starting with our parents, we've all been told, "dishonest people will not succeed in the long run." From business colleagues to bosses, students to teachers, and friends, most people you interact with, we hope, have the sense to see through manipulation.

Also, when people realize they have been tampered with by someone trying to take advantage of them, trust quickly goes out the window.

So, it's important to remember that honesty works both ways. You must first be trustworthy to gain the trust of others. But for others to be in your good graces, they too must earn your trust.

We grow up learning that nothing kills trust more than being caught in a lie. The first instinct when people are caught lying is to get defensive and try to talk themselves out of the situation they have created, which makes things even worse. That is not where you want to be, yet many people spent their time lying. Why is that you ask? Some of the research points to dishonesty as a result of avoiding pain at some level and psychologically speaking of course, this makes sense. Yet, you can't look at being honest, as a burden or a painful process. Look at honesty as an attribute you can be proud to own. Look at honesty as a benefit that will reward you. Think about this: if you promote honesty as a core value and foster it around you, you'll surround yourself with honest people. Since we know that psychologically we are attracted to people that are similar to ourselves, dishonest people will want to stay away, knowing you are a whistleblower when to comes to dishonesty.

They should assume that you are not the right person for them to be hanging around. For example, do drug dealers and thieves hang out or go near police officers or prosecutors? How much better will your life be knowing you don't have to worry about being surrounded by people who are lying and cheating? People want to follow honest and trustworthy leaders too. Those who embrace honesty and competence as top assets, are promotable. Here are some ways in which you can work on being trustworthy and honest:

Always keep an open mind: It's easy today to quickly come to a conclusion without facts or hear one side of the story and make an assumption. Practice keeping an open mind and do not quickly judge until you hear both sides and get all the facts. It's important to understand the other person's point of view, not just yours or the one you are defending.

Make real promises that you can keep: Back them up. Do not just give lip service to get what you want. Follow through. If you can't come through, you need to communicate that and ask what you can do to make the situation whole.

Be thoughtful and kind: People want to be treated nicely and so do you. Yes, it does take effort, but it's worth the reward and in making this a practice, it will become more automatic.

Set expectations: Since we use so much more non-verbal written communication today via email and texting, it's much easier for things to get lost in translation. Clarify what is being discussed and what the expectations are. Communication is key, make sure everyone is on the same page.

Making mistakes: Everyone makes mistakes. We are all human and life happens. Remember, it's ok to make mistakes, but it's not okay when you don't acknowledge and admit yours, or worse, you cover them up or lie about them.

The Art of the Win-Win

Have you ever heard people say they dealt with a situation and it was a win-win? The myth behind these stories supposes an either/or outcome—where everyone wins evenly or there is a big winner and a big loser. But in reality, when it comes to win-win deals there are three ways they happen. It looks like this: everyone walks away with something they wanted; there's one side that walks away the clear winner, and lastly, there are proven methods to becoming the primary winner.

Win-win as a negotiating philosophy has become more of a pop cliché in recent decades. Often people use it to describe how everyone wins. Even if one person ends up with only the scraps, you'll hear people mask it by saying "it was a win-win."

In reality one party is bound to get a little more in most scenarios. You can create a scenario where both sides win, but there are ways to make sure you are the bigger winner.

Knowing what you want: It may sound like a no-brainer, but you need to know what you want. Let's take a familiar example: you want to get a specific price on a used car. Your assumption is based on the supposed market value or the price you promised yourself you would not go above. The seller, meanwhile, wants to get a price but can't go any lower. If the price meets both of your needs it's a win-win. But often that does not happen.

This is where negotiations come in. Maybe you want some accessories for the car, such as seat covers or blue tooth speakers that are just sitting around in the seller's garage. You could ask if the items can be thrown into the deal. Therefore, you may pay a little more but you come out with something else you want, while he/she gets their price. That's a win-win.

Perhaps the seller can come down to your price if you have something, other than money, that you could offer, such as buying goods or services from your company, while you offer the person 20 percent off. Bartering is a good negotiating technique. In the example above, here are potential scenarios: let's say you own a hair salon and you know your buyer is interested in how their hair looks, you could offer x number of free haircuts. Likewise, if you run an auto body shop, you could offer x amount of free oil changes. There are ways you can create a win-win scenario that removes the financial equity component by utilizing the bartering system. You can use your expertise and provide services that are important to the person with whom you are making the deal. Using your skills and/or services can serve you well, especially in a world of financial strain.

When preparing yourself to enter into negotiations, learn to consider what matters to you. Take time to consider your priorities. This will clarify your real motives and interests. A good exercise is to take a piece of paper and draw a line down the middle. List all the things you want from the deal. Then on the other side contemplate how important each item is. Challenge yourself with these questions: "Does this really matter?" "Is it more important than the item listed above or below?" Then, take out another piece of paper and present yourself with multiple scenarios. Construct different offers and outcomes. What do they look like to you? These exercises will bring to light what matters most; which you can then prioritize from most important at the top to least important at the bottom.

Learn about the other side: When negotiating, it's vital to know the needs and goals of the other party. The earlier you know what they really want or need, the stronger your position and leverage. An effective way to gain understanding of the other side is to play devil's advocate. You can role play objectively to put the focus on the opposing team's potential interests instead of yours. In these exercises, eventually you want to satisfy your interests and the other side's interests as well.

If you've done this homework, you should come out of the negotiating process with the upper hand. It's important to note that, if you want to get all your needs met, at the expense of the other party getting nothing, it won't be in your best interest. It's been written time and again that even if you can get all the marbles for yourself, you need to give something to the other side. They need to satisfy some of their own needs and goals, too. This is all about being ethical in business, meeting your needs and theirs as well.

The essence and art of negotiation is not only about deal-making, it's about building relationships. It's important that the other side also feels like winners. It's even better if they do well because then you have an ally for future negotiations, whether it's buying a car or deciding who picks up the bill at dinner. If both people win (as in win-win) you get to improve the relationship.

Listening, asking the right questions, doing your homework, thinking outside the box: these are the assets in your toolbox that will help you be a winner time and again.

CONCLUSION

The start of the third decade of this century, brought us a pandemic, and with it, massive global disruptions the likes of which the world had not experienced since the last pandemic, when much of the world also experienced the disruption of World War I. But, for all the bad that has come, there are amazing opportunities that lie ahead for those who choose to embrace the future in a big way.

What does this mean for you? It means learning the soft skills to manage teams and organizing yourself in a way to expect disruption and transition, as we embark into the next iterations of digital communications and engagement, virtual working and most importantly, ethical, authentic and empowering professionals who take on leadership roles for the future of work. This means you have got to self-manage in a highly productive way. Consider all that you just learned in this book and how you can apply so much of this material as a hybrid or virtual team leader, leader-coach and or an advisor within your organization – wearing multiple hats on different teams. If you play your cards correctly, you will be playing many roles within your organization.

The skills and action-learning you are now actively developing by practicing and utilizing this book, as a coaching guide, will be with you for many years to come. Use the materials, exercises and learnings in this book, which will give you the skills and capabilities to manage in our new multi-generational decade as you continue to move up throughout your career and take on new leadership tasks and roles.

Build your career and stay well educated in all the current technologies, policies and procedures that are trending – because hyper speed demands this. Incorporate the lessons in this book, which are nimble and time tested, so they will continue to work for you, by adding your creative and reflective thinking.

Most importantly, this book is written so you can rely on yourself to get you to the top, with action-leadership development that is practical and time tested within the vast array of soft skills developments you just went through. Today there is a HUGE lack of mentoring skills amongst leaders; and therefore, the mentoring skill set is poised to become one of the most sought-after capabilities for executive management. So, my hope is that this book will stay with you as a guide to keep you on track as you grow in your career journey. I hope it will serve as a teacher and reference so you can overcome your obstacles, deal with difficult situations, environments and difficult people.

It is also my hope that you will read this book once a year, and as you do, you will contemplate your new goals and challenges, and how this book's instructions apply. *It's filled with tried-and-true principles, processes, methods and mannerisms that so many people lack today – THE SOFT SKILLS!*

Finally, LinkedIn.com and other survey companies have done polls regarding the top skills and organizational needs. For the past several years, the demand for people with talent in the soft skills arena, which include all the key leadership and mentoring skills that I discussed with you in this book, have been a top requirement. The most important lesson is that it's YOU - not the ever-changing technology systems - that will make you climb higher, and which will make companies perform and innovate better.

Wishing you longevity in your career,
Vinay Singh, MBA, Ed.M.

REFERENCES

Achstatter, Gerard. (Apr 21, 1999). "Succeed in Life, Ponder Your Death." *Investor's Business Daily*.

Achstatter, Gerard. (August 6, 1999). "Know, and Then Do." *Investor's Business Daily*.

Achstatter, Gerard. (December 22, 1998). "Urgent and Important Aren't the Same." *Investor's Business Daily*.

Achstatter, Gerard. (December, 11, 1999). "Read Your Way to the Top." *Investor's Business Daily*.

Achstatter, Gerard. (October, 16, 1998). "How to Put a Price on Your Learning." *Investor's Business Daily*.

Achstatter, Gerard. (September 22, 1998). "How to Avoid Decision-Making Errors." *Investor's Business Daily*.

Achstatter, Gerard. (September 23, 1998). "How to Add Hours to Your Busy Day." *Investor's Business Daily*.

Adams, Susan. (October 10, 2013). "Unhappy Employees Outnumber Happy Ones by Two to One Worldwide." *Forbes*. Retrieved from https://www.forbes.com/sites/susanadams/2013/10/10/unhappy-employees-outnumber-happy-ones-by-two-to-one-worldwide/#2f9413fb362a

Alexander, Amy Reynolds. (May 16, 2000). "Tips from the Wild on Details." *Investor's Business Daily*.

Computer and Commerce Association. Jack Ma: A Story of Success Through Failure" *ccamonash.com.au*

Cooper, Cord. (Apr 3, 2000). "Achieving Self Discipline." *Investor's Business Daily*.

Cooper, Cord. (April 13, 2000). "Going for the Win." *Investor's Business Daily.*

Cooper, Cord. (April 17, 2000). "Ending Procrastination." *Investor's Business Daily.*

Cooper, Cord. (April 27, 2000). "Smart Move: Focusing on Value." *Investor's Business Daily.*

Cooper, Cord. (July 2, 1999). "What Is Assertive Communication?" *Investor's Business Daily.*

Cooper, Cord. (July, 26,1999). "Forging Your Own Path." *Investor's Business Daily.*

Cooper, Cord. (June 14, 1999). "Going Over—And Around—Obstacles." *Investor's Business Daily.*

Cooper, Cord. (March 30, 1990). "Jordan, Evert On Positive Thought." *Investor's Business Daily.*

Cooper, Cord. (September, 21,1998). "Resilience Can Be Learned." *Investor's Business Daily.*

Gingerich, Mike. "Win over Your Audience: Be Confident While Presenting." *MikeGingerich.com.*

Jameson, Hunter. (October 5,1998). "Sound Support Can Help Your Persist." *Investor's Business Daily.*

Mimaroglu, Alp. (July 31,2017). "What Mark Cuban Learned From His 6 Biggest Failures." *Entrepreneur.com.*

Reynolds, Amy. (February 23, 2000) "The One-Minute Manager Redux." *Investor's Business Daily.*

Rister, Alex. "Presentation Lessons from Kevin Hart." *Creating Communications. alexrister1.wordpress.com*

Stockman-Vines, Linda. (September 9, 1999) "'Craziness' and Creativity." *Investor's Business Daily.*

Stockman-Vines, Linda. (December 3, 1998). "Are You Innovating Fast Enough?" *Investor's Business Daily.*

Stockman-Vines, Linda. (December 9, 1999). "CEOs Choose Stretch Polls". *Investor's Business Daily.*

Stockman-Vines, Linda. (March 25, 1999) "You Must Be Brave to Innovate." *Investor's Business Daily.*

Stockman-Vines, Linda. (September 9, 1999). "Innovate: Dare to Be Different." *Investor's Business Daily.*

Verveer, Melanie and Kim Azzarelli (October 6, 2015). "Fast Forward: How Women Can Achieve Power and Purpose." Mariner Books.

Wilkie, Dana. "Miserable Modern Workers: Why Are They So Unhappy?" Society for Human Resource Management. Retrieved from https://www.shrm.org/resourcesandtools/hr-topics/employee-relations/pages/employee-engagement-.aspx

CPSIA information can be obtained
at www.ICGtesting.com
Printed in the USA
LVHW021222310323
743129LV00003B/80/J